The Buddha's Victory

For thirty-five years Sangharakshita has been playing an important part in the spread of Buddhism throughout the modern world. He is head of the Western Buddhist Order (Trailokya Bauddha Mahasangha), and is actively engaged in what is now an international Buddhist movement with centres in thirteen countries worldwide. When not visiting centres he is based at a community in Norfolk. His writings are available in eleven languages.

Sangharakshita

The Buddha's Victory

Published by Windhorse Publications
136 Renfield Street
Glasgow G2 3AU

© Sangharakshita 1991

The cover was designed by Dhammarati using a thangka owned by the West
London Buddhist Centre

Printed on recycled paper by Biddles Ltd,
Guildford, Surrey

British Library Cataloguing in Publication Data
Sangharakshita, 1925—
The Buddha's victory.
1. Buddhism
I. Title
294.363

ISBN 0-904766-50-0

Publisher's note
Since this work is intended for a general readership, Pali and Sanskrit words
have been transliterated without the diacritical marks which would have been
appropriate in a work of a more scholarly nature.

Contents

Editor's Introduction

The Buddha was not a god, nor was he the incarnation of a god. He was born a human being, the son of the king of a small state on the borders of contemporary India and Nepal. His life was a human life, his achievement a human one—even if it did significantly expand the meaning of the word 'human'.

And yet two-and-a-half-thousand years have passed since the Buddha walked on Earth; there are no records to suggest that he or any of his closest disciples could read or write; and his impact, not only on the people he taught, but on their followers, and on their followers' followers, was such that his historical, human, essence was soon, and understandably, exalted by an aura of myth and legend. Within a few hundred years the heirs to the Buddha's teaching would be choosing for themselves whether to visualize him as a rag-apparelled mendicant walking the dusty pathways of northern India, or as semi-divine being, eternally youthful, eternally preaching his transcendental message from the heights of the Vulture's Peak.

For his modern day successors, especially those who live in the West, the stock of images is almost bewilderingly rich. With the entire Buddhist tradition at his or her disposal, the contemporary Buddhist cannot even acquire a statuette of the Buddha without having to decide whether to choose one with Indian, Chinese, Burmese, Thai, Japanese, Tibetan, or even Western features.

There is really nothing wrong with this; indeed, this abundance of choices provides a graphic testimony to the effectiveness with which the Buddha's teaching has not only spread throughout the world, but burrowed its way into the collective psyche of its successive host-cultures. The Buddha was an ideal human being; it is therefore only to be expected that he should have become idealized over time.

Nevertheless, as human beings struggling to embody the ideals that he represents in the everyday world that we inhabit, we may well feel the need to meet and engage with the Buddha, not just in his idealized form, but in his human form too. If he was a human being who, through effort and insight, made ideals a reality, then we will only gain by getting to know him on a down-to-earth, human, level. What obstacles did he have to overcome in order to gain Enlightenment? Did he find it easy to convince others that he had something to offer? What sort of issues were on his mind as he organized his first disciples into a coherent spiritual community? And how did he face death?

If we would like an encounter with the Buddha in this aspect, then it is to the Pali texts that we must turn. Committed to writing long after the Buddha's lifetime, they are probably less historically exact, and certainly less of an unshakeable foundation for any kind of Buddhist 'orthodoxy', than some may like to claim. But the Buddha we meet in their pages—energetic, kindly, confident, sharp-witted, and urbane—is a multi-faceted, attractive, and above all believable character: he is the ideal made flesh. In the ancient Pali accounts the Buddha glows, rather than dazzles, with all the warmth, wit, and charm of a living, thinking, communicating person. He is a full-bloodied historical figure. And if the world of the Pali Canon, with its gods, devas, Maras, and occasional miracles, is just a little more magical than our own, then most of us, I am sure, will feel enchanted and attracted rather than excluded and repelled. The invitation to walk and talk with the Buddha calls to us from its pages with an irresistible force.

Having entered that world, having met and listened to the Buddha, our next task is one of reflection and imagination. We have to try to work out exactly why the Buddha gave a certain teaching at a particular time, what was its precise relevance to the spiritual development of his followers of the time, and what relevance it might have for us today. This is not always easy, nor is it always as comforting as we might hope. What was the true content of the Buddha's first discourse? Why did he think so hard before allowing women to join his Order? Why did he seem to shrug off a devotional offering of flowers? The Buddha's teaching may be a 'personal invitation', but it is not an invitation to follow blindly or to pay lip-service to a set of rules and dogmas: it is an invitation to contemplate, to meditate, and to test in our own experience. True, by entering the world of the scriptures we get a chance to sit at the Buddha's feet; but we sit there so that, in time, we will get up and act, so that we will go out and transform ourselves.

In the five talks that form the basis of this book, Sangharakshita takes us into that world, and shares with us some of his own reflections and conclusions. In performing such an exercise, of course, one could argue that he runs the risk of doing our thinking for us, of cramping rather than stimulating our own attempts to form an imaginative link with the Buddha and his world. But fear not; Sangharakshita's interpretations and reflections are communicated with all the energy and devotion of his own quest for truth and higher values. Not only do they provide us with a galvanizing example of a committed approach to 'scripture-study', but they also have the virtue of posing as many questions as they answer. This book will make you think very hard about yourself, your life, and your goals.

All of these talks were given on 'home ground', in the context of gatherings organized either by the Friends of the Western Buddhist Order (FWBO), the now world-wide Movement that Sangharakshita founded in 1967, or the Western Buddhist Order (WBO) itself, the spiritual community that he established in 1968. To the outside observer, therefore, these pages also provide a glimpse of Sangharakshita as a preceptor, a man deploying as skilfully as he can the fruits of his own encounter with the Buddha in the service of the community whose development he is trying to encourage. Is the FWBO/WBO therefore 'his' Movement, as is sometimes suggested, or—thanks to him—a fitting new branch of the Buddha's sangha? Perhaps the following pages will help you to decide.

Nagabodhi
Vimalakula Community
May 1991

The Buddha's Victory

For a Buddhist, the highest values of existence are incarnated in three great ideals. Firstly, there is the ideal of Enlightenment, the ideal of the perfectly developed human being. Secondly, there is the ideal of the path to Enlightenment, the sum total of all the principles, practices, and teachings that help the individual human being in the course of his or her quest for spiritual perfection. Thirdly, there is the ideal of fellowship in pursuing the way to Enlightenment. By this is meant the deriving of encouragement, help, inspiration, and stimulus, from other individuals who are also trying to perfect themselves. In traditional terms, these three great ideals are embodied in the Buddha, the Dhamma, and the Sangha.

The Buddha embodies the ideal of Enlightenment. The word *Buddha* means 'the Enlightened One', humanity perfected. The Dhamma, the truth, doctrine, or teaching of the Buddha, embodies the path. The Sangha, the spiritual community of those who follow the path and study and practise the teaching, embodies the fellowship of those treading the Way.

These three are known in traditional Buddhist terms as the Three Jewels. They are also known as the Three Refuges or the Triple Gem, or even, in the Chinese tradition, as the Three Treasures. Between them they represent the highest values and ideals of Buddhism. However widely Buddhism has spread over the centuries, however richly it has developed in various ways, everything relates to one or another of these three, or to all of them jointly. Anything that is not connected with the Buddha, the Dhamma, or the Sangha, has no real connection with Buddhism at all.

Like all spiritual traditions Buddhism has two aspects: a 'popular' aspect, the aspect of ordinary, everyday practice and observance, and a 'philosophical' aspect, which is concerned with the deeper understanding of the teaching. The popular aspect includes such things as festivals and celebrations. If we look at the Buddhist calendar we see that Buddhism has quite a large number of festivals and celebrations of various kinds. These vary a little from one part of the Buddhist world to another, but the most important are common to all parts of the Buddhist world. Of all these festivals the three most important are all associated with the Three Jewels.

Jewels are generally considered to be the most precious of all material things, while the Buddha, Dhamma, and Sangha are considered to be the most precious of all non-material things. Because they are so precious, we rejoice to have them; they give meaning and purpose to our lives, and give orientation to everything we do.

But it is not easy to rejoice all the time, or even to be aware of our good fortune all the time. Tradition has therefore set aside these three days in the year—all full moon days—on which we make a special effort to remember and rejoice in the Three Jewels. Thus on the full moon day of May we rejoice in the Buddha jewel, on the full moon day of July we rejoice in the Dhamma jewel, and on the full moon day of November we rejoice in the Sangha jewel. The fact that these festivals fall on full moon days, incidentally, is not accidental. It indicates our need to maintain a harmony between ourselves and nature. It reminds us that however far we progress along the path of the 'higher evolution', we we must not lose contact with the recurrent rhythms of the 'lower evolution'.

Today is the day on which we rejoice in the Buddha

jewel. In particular this means that it is the day on which
we rejoice in the Buddha's attainment of Enlightenment,
rejoice in what it was that actually made the Buddha a
Buddha.

We usually call this day Buddha Day, but it is sometimes
known as Wesak. *Wesak*, a Sinhalese word, is actually a
corruption of the Indian word *Vaishaka*, which is in turn
short for *Vaishaka purnima*, which means 'the full moon day
of April-to-May'. In India, especially, Buddha Day is often
referred to as *Buddha jayanti*, *jayanti* coming from the word
jaya, meaning 'victory'. *Buddha jayanti* therefore means the
celebration of the 'Buddha's victory'. But what is this
victory?

Victory usually implies victory *over* someone or something. Who or what, then, could this have been in the
Buddha's case? The answer is simple: the Buddha conquered Mara, the 'Evil One', and after conquering Mara,
attained Enlightenment. In a sense, his conquest of Mara,
his *Mara-vijaya* as it is called, *was* his attainment of
Enlightenment.

It is possible that you have already encountered descrip-
tions of the episode of the conquest of Mara. Perhaps you
have seen it depicted in Buddhist art. If so, you will have
seen the Buddha-to-be sitting on a heap of kusa grass
beneath the spreading branches of the *ficus religiosus*, or
sacred fig tree—subsequently known, in honour of the
Buddha, as the Bodhi tree, or 'tree of Enlightenment'. He
is surrounded on all sides by thousands of fearsome
figures, all horribly misshapen and deformed. Some of
them are whirling enormous clubs, some are spitting fire;
some are in the act of hurling great rocks, even whole
mountains that they have torn up by the roots; some again
are discharging arrows. These are the forces of Mara. Mara
himself stands to one side directing his terrible army in its
onslaught on the Buddha. But the Buddha himself takes no

notice. He is completely surrounded by an aura of golden light. As soon as the various missiles touch this aura they turn into flowers and fall to the ground at the Buddha's feet as though in unintentional worship. The Buddha is undisturbed and carries on meditating. He does not take any notice even when Mara summons his three daughters and orders them to dance in the most seductive manner. So Mara retires defeated, his forces disappear, and his three daughters withdraw in confusion. The Buddha is left alone beneath the Bodhi tree on his heap of kusa grass, and carries on meditating. Sitting there in that way he attains Enlightenment.

Such is the well known episode. But like other well known episodes in the Buddha's life it is open to misunderstanding. We might of course realize that the episode is symbolic, but we may not understand that the episode of the *Mara-vijaya* was not the only episode of its kind to occur in the Buddha's life; may not understand that this was not the Buddha's *only* victory.

Far from being his only victory the *Mara-vijaya* represented the culmination of an entire series of victories. This is only to be expected, because spiritual life is like that. One does not develop the fullness of wisdom all at once or the fullness of compassion all at once. One does not develop the fullness of energy and heroism necessary to defeat Mara and his forces all at once. One does not develop any spiritual quality all at once; one develops it gradually. As the Buddha himself said in the *Dhammapada*: 'As a pot becomes full by the constant falling of drops of water, so, little by little, does a man fill himself with good.'

'*Little by little*'. Before the Buddha's great victory there will have been many lesser victories, victories without which the great victory could hardly have taken place. We shall now consider some of those lesser victories—victories that are such only in relation to the *great* victory over Mara.

In themselves, these lesser victories are such as we might find hard even to imagine.

The Buddha's first victory, so far as we know at least, is generally described as the 'Going Forth' from home into homelessness. We may not be accustomed to considering this as a victory, but that is what it was. Just suppose that you were the son or daughter of wealthy parents, with high social position and great prestige. Suppose you were young, healthy, and good looking. Suppose too that you were happily married, perhaps with a child.... Would *you* have found it easy to give it all up? Would you have been able to 'go forth' for the sake of you knew not what—for the sake of the 'truth', for the sake of something 'higher', something beyond anything you had yet experienced or imagined? This is exactly what Siddhartha, the Buddha-to-be, actually did.

There are several accounts of what happened on that occasion, some of them very colourful and romantic. They describe, for instance, how Siddhartha drew aside a curtain in the inner apartments of his palace and took his last long, lingering look at his peacefully sleeping wife and infant son. They describe how the gods of the various heavens silently opened the gates so that he could depart unseen and unheard. And they describe how those same gods supported the hooves of his horse on the palms of their hands so that there would be no noise.... But the oldest account is actually very simple. Reminiscing in his old age, the Buddha simply said to his disciples:

'Then I, monks, after a time, being young, my hair coal-black, possessed of radiant youth, in the prime of my life—although my unwilling parents wept and wailed—having cut off my hair and beard, having put on yellow robes, went forth from home into homelessness.*

Whether the description is elaborate or simple, what actually happened is sufficiently clear. The Buddha-to-be left home. He left his family, left the *group*.

But in what sense was this a victory? What was it a victory *over*? It was a victory over the family, or rather, over the *group* as represented especially by his parents. The Buddha himself once said that he went forth 'against the wishes' of his weeping parents.

But this was also a victory in a deeper sense. It was a victory over his *attachment* to the group. It could not have been easy for Siddhartha to leave his family; his actual departure must have been preceded by a long internal struggle. But in the end he broke free from the group. This did not just mean leaving the group physically: it meant overcoming group attitudes and group conditioning; it meant taking the initiative, doing something that he wanted to do; it meant thinking for himself, experiencing things for himself; it meant living his own life; it meant being an *individual*. Thus the 'Going Forth' from home into homelessness was a victory over the 'internalized' group.

Having gone forth from home into homelessness, Siddhartha approached two famous spiritual teachers. These teachers, who seem to have been good and noble men, taught the Buddha everything they knew, taught him what they believed to be the highest truth. Siddhartha was a very good pupil, and learned what they had to teach. Whatever they taught him, he experienced for himself, very quickly becoming their equal. Realizing this, they offered to share with him the leadership of the communities they had founded. But he refused and, leaving

---

* *Majjhima Nikaya I (Middle Length Sayings)*, Ariyapariyesana Sutta, trans. I.B. Horner, Pali Text Society, London, 1967, p. 207

them, returned to his solitary wanderings.

This too was a victory, a victory over spiritual complacency and spiritual ambition. Siddhartha had experienced for himself everything that his teachers had to teach, but he knew that there was still something 'beyond', something higher which he had not yet realized—and which he wanted to realize. He knew that he was not yet fully Enlightened, despite what his teachers were telling him. In other words, he did not settle down with a limited spiritual experience—even though by ordinary standards it was quite a high experience. It was not the highest, and the Buddha *knew* that it was not the highest. In this way he overcame spiritual complacency. Moreover, his teachers had offered to share with him the leadership of their communities. What an opportunity was this for a young man! But Siddhartha refused. He was not concerned with leadership. He was concerned with *truth*, he was concerned with *Enlightenment*. In this way he overcame spiritual ambition.

It is interesting to note that Siddhartha overcame spiritual complacency and spiritual ambition at the same time. The two are actually closely connected. If you are spiritually ambitious, in the sense of seeking a position of spiritual leadership, you are likely to become spiritually complacent. Similarly, if you are spiritually complacent, you will tend to seek a position of spiritual leadership by way of compensation for your lack of real spiritual effort.

Continuing his quest alone, Siddhartha decided to live in the depths of the forest, far from any human habitation. He lived somewhere where it was very difficult to live, even for those committed to the spiritual life. Furthermore, he stayed in what we would call 'haunted' places, places inhabited, at least according to popular belief, by ghosts and spirits—places in which feelings of fear and terror were likely to arise. And those feelings of panic, fear, and terror *did* arise in his mind. So what did Siddhartha do on these occasions? If the fear and terror arose while he was walking to and fro, he continued walking to and fro until he had overcome them. He did not run away, did not try to escape from those feelings. Similarly, if they arose while he was sitting still, or while he was lying down, then that is where he faced and overcame them. In this way he was victorious over fear.

Even today, of course, many people have this experience of fear and terror, panic and dread—or of anxiety at least—especially when they are alone. But howsoever and wheresoever we have this sort of experience, it is important to face it. It is important not to run away, whether literally or metaphorically. If we face it we will eventually overcome it, as Siddhartha did.

Even though Siddhartha had overcome fear, he had still not attained Enlightenment. He now embarked upon a course of extreme 'self-mortification'. The Buddhist scriptures give us full details of the various torments that he inflicted upon himself. Suffice it to say that he subsequently asserted that no one had gone to such extremes of self-mortification as had he. Indeed, he very nearly died. But there were compensations. He became famous. In those days it was popularly believed that you could attain Enlightenment by means of self-mortification—the more extreme the better. He therefore attracted, in particular, five close disciples, who intended to remain with him until, as a result of his self-mortification, he attained Enlightenment.

But Siddhartha did not attain Enlightenment in this way. Apparently, he remained as far from Enlightenment as ever. He therefore gave up self-mortification, even though he had been practising it for years, and—to the shock of his disciples—started taking solid food again. The five disciples left him immediately, deeply disappointed that he was not the man they had thought him to be. He had weakened, they thought, and had returned to a life of luxury. Once again Siddhartha was left alone.

On the face of it this might look like a defeat, but it was actually a great victory. On this instance Siddhartha had overcome the very human tendency to refuse to admit that one has made a mistake, that one has been on the wrong path, and that one must now retrace one's steps and start all over again. After all, when one has invested a great deal of energy, not to speak of time, money, and all sorts of other things, in making that mistake, one does not like to admit, even to oneself, that all the effort has in a sense been wasted. But Siddhartha did not mind doing this. He did not mind losing his disciples, he did not mind being on his own again. It would have been easy, in comparison, to continue with his self-mortification, easy to become more and more famous, easy to attract great numbers of disciples. But instead he admitted that he had made a mistake, and continued his quest.

Eventually, his quest took him to the foot of the Bodhi tree. There he sat down, as we have seen, and was attacked by Mara and his forces.

But who, or what, is Mara? I have already described this episode as it is depicted in Buddhist art, but I must now pay some attention to its *significance*—even though the symbolic terms in which the episode is described do actually communicate their own message. If we do not understand what Mara represents, we will not be able to understand the true significance of the Buddha's *Maravijaya*, his victory over Mara.

The word *mara* means 'killing', 'destroying', it means bringing death and pestilence. Mara is therefore the principle of destruction. Sometimes this principle is personified, and thus it happens that the Buddhist texts mention no less than *four* Maras. These are (in Pali) *Maccumara*, *Khandhamara*, *Kilesamara*, and *Devaputtamara*. We will look at each

21

of them in turn.

First of all comes *Maccumara*. Here, Mara simply means 'death' or 'destruction'. Death, of course, is usually very unwelcome. Sometimes people are really surprised when it comes, even though they should have known it was coming all the time. Because death is so unwelcome, people tend to regard it as an evil. But in itself death is neither good nor evil: it is just a fact of existence and has to be recognized. That is what *Maccumara* actually represents.

Secondly, rather more metaphysically, there is *Khandhamara*. This Mara represents a sort of extension of *Maccumara*. Here we remember that death is not just an abstraction, not just a word. Death is a concrete reality. Death means that there are *things* and *beings* which die, which are destroyed. And these things and beings which die between them constitute a world. In other words, there is a world which is under the sway of death. This is the world of what are called the *khandhas,* in Pali (Sanskrit *skandhas*). These *khandhas,* or 'aggregates', as the word is often translated, are five in number. First of all there is *rupa*, or material form, then *vedana*, or feeling, then *samjna*, or perception, then *sankara*, or volition, and finally *vijnana*, or consciousness. These five *khandhas* are well known; if you know anything at all about Buddhism you will be familiar with them. Between them these five *khandhas* represent the whole of conditioned existence, the whole of mundane existence, the whole of 'relative reality', or, in more traditional terms, the whole of the *samsara*. That is what *Khandhamara* represents.

Thirdly, there is *Kilesamara*. *Kilesa* comes from a root meaning 'to adhere' or 'to stick to', and is cognate with the word for 'slime'. *Kilesa* means 'stain', 'soil', or 'impurity'. In an ethical sense it means 'depravity', 'lust', or 'passion'. Broadly speaking, *kilesa* corresponds to what is otherwise called *akusalacitta* or *akusalacittani*, or 'unskilful mental states'. The five principal *kilesas*, or 'defilements', as they are generally called in English, are generally enumerated as craving, aversion, ignorance, conceit, and distraction. The first three of these—craving, aversion, and ignorance —correspond to the three *akusalamulas* or 'roots of unskilfulness', which are represented by the cock, the snake, and the pig that we see at the centre of the Tibetan Wheel of Life. It is these three that keep the wheel turning. In other words, it is because our minds are dominated by the *kilesas* that we are reborn within the *samsara*, reborn in the world of conditioned existence, the world that is under the sway of death. This is what *Kilesamara* represents.

And then there is *Devaputtamara*. *Deva* means 'god', with a small G, and *putta* means 'son'. So *Devaputta* means 'son of a god', which is to say, a god—just as 'son of man' means a man. *Devaputtamara* is Mara as an actually existing being or person. He is the being who appears in the episode of the Buddha's *Mara-vijaya*. Sometimes *Devaputtamara* is regarded as being simply a personification of the *kilesas* or defilements, but *Devaputtamara* cannot really be reduced in this way. Naturally he is dominated by the defilements, just as are most beings within the *samsara*; but at the same time he has his own being and position in the universe. He has his own place in Buddhist mythology.

Buddhism sees the universe as consisting of various planes and worlds. These are the objective counterparts— or correlatives—of mental states, both positive and negative. Just as there is a 'world' of human beings, according to Buddhist cosmology, so also is there a 'world' of animals, a 'world' of gods, a 'world' of demons, and so on. Mara belongs to one of these worlds, in fact to one of the lower heaven worlds. Low though it is, however, Mara rules over this world; indeed, he rules over all the worlds belonging to what is called the *kamaloka*, or 'realm of sensuous desire', which includes our own human world. In a wider sense, of course, Mara rules over the entire universe, the whole of conditioned existence—because it is subject to *death*, which Mara primarily represents. But he rules particularly over the *kamaloka*, or realm of sensuous desire.

In order to understand why this should be we must first realize that above the realm of sensuous desire there is the *rupaloka* or 'realm of archetypal form'. This realm corresponds to the various mental states of higher meditative consciousness. From these states, from the *rupaloka*, it is possible to gain Enlightenment—which it is not possible to do from the *kamaloka*. Mara is therefore particularly anxious to stop people reaching the *rupaloka*, that is, stop them escaping from the *kamaloka*. This is why Mara, with the help of his forces and his daughters, tried to interrupt the Buddha's meditation beneath the Bodhi tree. Perhaps he sometimes tries to interrupt *your* meditation. Perhaps that little distraction which arises in your mind, perhaps even that little tickling sensation that distracts you, is none other than Mara.

Perhaps I have said enough about Mara to place us in a better position to understand what it was that the Buddha actually conquered. We can now return to the *Mara-vijaya* itself. As we have seen, there are four *Maras*: *Maccumara*, *Khandhamara*, *Kilesamara*, and *Devaputtamara*. The Buddha overcame all four of them; his victory was therefore a fourfold victory. Let us look at each of them in turn.

How did the Buddha overcome *Maccumara*? How did he overcome death? He overcame death by overcoming *birth*, for where there is birth there will inevitably be death. He overcame birth by overcoming the unskilful mental states that lead to birth—that is to say to *rebirth*. In other words, the Buddha overcame death by attaining what in Pali is called the *amatapada*, the 'deathless state', the state which is free from death, free from birth—that is, Nibbana. He overcame death by attaining Enlightenment, a state which is above and beyond conditioned existence. It is not that after attaining Enlightenment the Buddha could not be reborn in the human world if he wanted to be. But he would not be reborn there *out of compulsion*, as a result of previous *kamma* (Sanskrit *karma*) that he had committed. He would be reborn—if he was reborn at all—out of compassion, in order to continue to help ordinary, unenlightened human beings.

How did the Buddha overcome *Khandhamara*? How did he overcome conditioned existence? He overcame conditioned existence by overcoming the *kilesas*, the defilements, which lead one into conditioned existence. He overcame the *kilesas* at the time that he attained Enlightenment. In a sense, the two things were synonymous. According to tradition, however, the Buddha did not finally overcome the *khandhas* until his *parinibbana* forty-five years later. At the time of his *parinibbana* he severed all connection with the physical body, severed all connection with the *khandhas*. For this reason the *parinibbana* is also known as *khandhanibbana*, or *anupadisesanibbana*, that is to say, 'Nibbana without remainder in the form of a physical body'.

But how *did* the Buddha overcome the *kilesas*? So much depends upon this. As we have seen, there are five principal *kilesas*: craving, aversion, ignorance, conceit, and distraction. The Buddha overcame craving by means of tranquillity, aversion by means of friendliness and compassion, ignorance by means of wisdom, conceit by means of selflessness, and distraction by means of awareness, or mindfulness. Naturally, it was not easy even for the Buddha to do this. Tranquillity, friendliness, compassion, and so on do not just appear—not even when one is seated beneath the Bodhi tree! They have to be developed. But they *can* be developed. Indeed, the fact that they can be developed is one of the central teachings of Buddhism. It is one of the central teachings of Buddhism that our mental states are in our own power and can be changed. Furthermore, Buddhism not only exhorts us to change them, but also tells us just *how* to do this; it gives us specific meditation 'methods'.

Tranquillity is developed by means of the three 'contemplations': the contemplation of the repulsiveness of the physical body, the contemplation of death, and the contemplation of impermanence.

The first of these, the contemplation of the repulsiveness of the physical body, is the most extreme, and generally takes the form of actually contemplating the ten stages in the progressive decomposition of a corpse. Perhaps I should add that it is usually taught only to those who are psychologically and spiritually mature. The other two are less extreme and are therefore taught more widely. But whichever method we practise, whether the contemplation of death or the contemplation of impermanence, or even the contemplation of the repulsiveness of the physical body, we can succeed in developing tranquillity. And by developing tranquillity we overcome craving.

We develop friendliness and compassion by means of *Metta Bhavana*, or the 'cultivation of universal loving-kindness'. This practice consists in the systematic development of goodwill towards oneself, towards a near and dear friend, towards a 'neutral' person, towards an 'enemy', and, finally, towards all living beings. The *Metta Bhavana* is one of the best known and most popular of all Buddhist meditation methods. By practising it we can succeed in developing friendliness and compassion, and by developing friendliness and compassion we overcome aversion.

We can develop wisdom by means of the contemplation of the twelve *nidanas*, or 'links'. For a detailed discussion of these, I must refer readers to my other writings (in particular *A Survey of Buddhism* and *The Three Jewels*).

Broadly speaking, we develop wisdom by reflecting on the conditionality of mundane existence, on the fact that whatever mundane phenomenon arises or comes into existence does so in dependence on certain definite causes and conditions. Reflection on the conditionality of mundane existence is also roughly tantamount to reflecting on *sunnata* or 'voidness'. In these different ways we develop wisdom, and by developing wisdom we overcome ignorance.

We develop selflessness by reflection on the six 'elements'. The six elements are earth, water, fire, air, space, and consciousness. In this practice we reflect that there exists in our own physical body the element *earth* in the form of flesh, bone, and so on. We then further reflect that the earth element in our physical body does not really belong to us. We may point to our bodies and say 'this is me', 'this is mine'; but it does *not* belong to us. The earth element within our physical bodies has been borrowed, literally borrowed, from the earth element in the universe. One day we shall have to give it back. If we see a corpse— even the corpse of a little bird—in the process of decomposition, we can actually see this happening, especially if the corpse is lying on the earth. We can see the flesh and bone that once belonged to the body returning to the soil, returning to the earth, returning to the earth element in the universe from which it came. Similarly, one day, we too shall have to give our body back to the earth element. We should therefore not be attached to it. We should not identify with it by saying 'this body belongs to me'. We then continue to reflect in this way with regard to all of the six elements. As we do so, we develop selflessness, and by developing selflessness we overcome conceit.

Finally, we develop mindfulness, or awareness, by means of *anapanasati*, or the 'recollection of breathing'. Here we simply 'watch' our breath, without interfering with it in any way, allowing our minds to be increasingly focused, increasingly concentrated on the breath. By practising *anapanasati* we develop mindfulness, and by developing mindfulness we overcome distraction, overcome the wandering mind.

Thus the five principal *kilesas* are overcome by these methods of meditation. This is how the Buddha overcame them. He overcame craving by means of tranquillity, aversion by means of friendliness and compassion, ignorance by means of wisdom, conceit by means of selflessness, and distraction by means of mindfulness, or awareness. In this way the Buddha overcame *Kilesamara*.

There is one Mara left. How did the Buddha overcome *Devaputtamara*, or 'Mara the son of a god'? To understand this we must return to the episode of the *Maravijaya*, or victory over Mara, as depicted in Buddhist art.

In the traditional representations of this incident we see the Buddha seated beneath the Bodhi tree, his eyes closed, or half closed, and we see Mara with his forces and his daughters. The Buddha is not paying Mara any attention at all. We could therefore say that the Buddha overcame *Devaputtamara* simply by ignoring him.

In ordinary life, of course, to ignore someone usually means that we have a rather negative attitude towards them. But the Buddha could not possibly have had a negative attitude towards anyone—not even towards Mara. So we must try to put things a little more positively. It is not so much that the Buddha ignored Mara: rather, he overcame Mara simply *by being himself*. He overcame him by being the Bodhisatta, by being the Buddha. According to the medieval Indian commentator Mallinatha, the word *jayati*, or 'to conquer', means to surpass everything else by means of one's own excellence. It means to be the 'highest'. Thus the Buddha's victory over Mara was not the result of a fight *on Mara's terms*; he defeated Mara simply by being

himself, by virtue of the sheer excellence of his moral and
spiritual qualities.

Thus the Buddha's victory over Mara was complete.
Because it was complete he attained Enlightenment. One
would have thought, therefore, that there was nothing left
for him to do, nothing left for him to overcome. In a sense
this is true, but after the *Maravijaya* there is in fact another
episode, an episode that represents yet another victory,
perhaps the ultimate victory. This is the episode of
Brahma's request. Let us now witness it in our mind's eye:

The Buddha has attained Enlightenment; he is enjoying
the freedom and bliss of Enlightenment. He is also reflecting that the truth he has discovered is very deep indeed,
and therefore very difficult to understand. As he reflects in
this way he is inclined not to try to communicate this
truth—the Dhamma—to other human beings: it will be just
too difficult. After all, he reflects, beings are deeply immersed in worldly pleasures, they will not be able to understand the Dhamma he has discovered. Just then,
Brahmasahampati, another figure from Buddhist mythology, the 'Lord of a Thousand Worlds', appears. He
pleads with the Buddha, pointing out that there are at least
a few beings who *will* understand. He implores that for
their sake the Buddha should communicate the truth he
has discovered. In the end the Buddha agrees, saying:
'Opened for those who hear are the doors of the Deathless,
Brahma, let them give forth their faith.'[*]

Here, the Buddha has overcome the temptation to keep
his Enlightenment to himself, or even to think that he *could*
keep it to himself. He has overcome spiritual individualism. The Buddha has overcome the Buddha—and has
therefore become truly the Buddha. This is the last and
greatest of all his victories. He has overcome the group,

---

[*] *Ibid.* p. 213

including the internalized group. He has overcome spiritual complacency and spiritual ambition. He has overcome fear. He has overcome the tendency to refuse to admit that he has made a mistake. He has overcome all four Maras. Now, finally, he has overcome spiritual individualism. He has been victorious all along the line. He is not only the Buddha, not only the Enlightened One, but he is also the *Jina*, the 'Victorious One'.

In the West we are accustomed to using the title 'Buddha'. But we should not forget that the Buddha is also commonly known as the *Jina*. Similarly, followers of the Buddha are usually called 'Buddhists', but perhaps they could just as easily be called 'Jinists': followers of the *Jina*, the Victorious One. The Buddha did in fact once tell his disciples that they were *ksatriyas*, or 'warriors', fighting for *sila*, fighting for *samadhi*, fighting for *panna*. They were fighting to live an ethical life, fighting for higher states of consciousness, and fighting for transcendental wisdom. According to the Buddha, the spiritual life is an active life, a strenuous life. We might even say that it is a *militant* life. We have to take the offensive against Mara. We should not wait for him to come and tap us on the shoulder. Attack is the best method of defence, prevention is better than cure.

For this reason, Western Buddhists should beware of taking too soft a view of the spiritual life. Perhaps we do not meditate hard enough, study hard enough, work hard enough, even play hard enough. Perhaps we have not committed ourselves to the Three Jewels with sufficient depth and intensity. Perhaps we do not really want to spread the Dhamma. Perhaps we are just playing at being Buddhists. If that is the case then we will not get very far: we will not be truly successful or genuinely happy. We will not be real Buddhists, and we certainly won't be real *Jinists*, real spiritual warriors.

Nowadays there is so much to be overcome, both in

ourselves and in the world. There is so much to be trans-
formed by the 'Golden Light'. As the life of the Buddha
reminds us, we have to overcome the group; we have to
overcome spiritual complacency and spiritual ambition;
we have to overcome fear; we have to overcome that very
human tendency to refuse to admit that we have made a
mistake; we have to overcome Mara; and we have to overcome spiritual individualism. In short, we have to overcome everything that the Buddha overcame so that we can
attain Enlightenment just as he did, and benefit the world
just as he benefited it.

This is certainly not easy, and no real Buddhist has ever
said that it was. But a human being should be ashamed not
to attempt that which is difficult rather than easy. A human
being should be ashamed not to attempt that which is the
most difficult of all. A human being should be ashamed not
to be fighting against the odds. Sometimes we may feel that
we are being overwhelmed. We may feel that we are
having to hack our way through a dense jungle: the jungle
of *samsara*, the jungle of conditioned existence. The Buddha
must have felt like that too at times. After his Enlightenment he gave some of his disciples the following parable:

'Just as if, brethren, a man travelling in a forest, along
a mountain height, should come upon an ancient
road, an ancient track, traversed by men of former
days, and should proceed along it: and as he went
should come upon an old-time city, a royal city of
olden days, dwelt in by men of bygone ages, laid out
with parks and groves and water tanks, and stoutly
walled about—a delightful spot.

Then suppose, brethren, that this man should tell
of his find to the king or royal minister, thus: "Pardon
me, sire, but I would have you know that while
travelling in a forest, along a mountain height, I came

upon an ancient road, an ancient track, traversed by
men of former days, and proceeded along it. And as
I went I came upon an old-time city, a royal city of
olden days, dwelt in by men of bygone ages, laid out
with parks and groves and water tanks, and stoutly
walled about, a delightful spot. Sire, restore that city"

Then suppose, brethren, that king or royal minister
were to restore that city, so that thereafter it became
prosperous, fortunate, and populous, crowded with
inhabitants, and were to reach growth and increase.

Even so, brethren, have I seen an ancient Path, an
ancient track traversed by the Perfectly Enlightened
ones of former times. And what is that Path? It is this
Ariyan Eightfold Path.'[*]

This parable tells us a number of things. It tells us that the
Buddha was a pioneer. It tells us that the state of Enlightenment is like a wonderful city inhabited by innumerable
people. It tells us that there is a way to that city, a way to
that state. Above all, however, the parable reminds us that
the Buddha's teaching is something that can be lost. The
Three Jewels can be lost. Values can be lost. Fortunately,
we are living at a time and in a place where the Dhamma
is still known, and can still be practised. We can still tread
the ancient road to the city. But the jungle has started to
encroach. Fewer people now live in the city; parts of the
city are in a derelict condition, and entire sections of the
road are overgrown.

Even though we are not being called upon to be pioneers
in the way that the Buddha was, there is still a lot for us to
do. We have to hack away at the jungle; we have to be
spiritual warriors; we have to be not just Buddhists, but
Jinists: we have at least to make an effort to overcome what

---

[*] Sutta Nipata ii, 103–4, from *Some Sayings of the Buddha* trans. F.L.
Woodward, Oxford University Press, London, 1939

the Buddha overcame. If we are not prepared to make that effort, then we are not worthy to celebrate Buddha Day, not worthy to celebrate *Buddha jayanti*, not worthy to celebrate the Buddha's victory.

The New Man Speaks

Two months ago, on the full moon night of the Indian month *Vaishaka*, we celebrated the Buddha's attainment of Enlightenment. Tonight, we are celebrating 'Dhamma-cakka Day', or, to give it its full title, '*Dhammacakkappavattana* Day', the day commemorating the 'setting in motion of the Wheel of the Dhamma'—this being the traditional Buddhist idiom for the Buddha's initial promulgation of the truth that he had realized at the time of his Enlightenment. On this occasion, having gained Enlightenment, the Buddha brought out into the open, in the form of words and thoughts, the content of his transcendental realization on the night of *Vaishaka purnima*.

Two months ago we left the Buddha sitting cross-legged on a heap of grass at the foot of the Bodhi tree, enjoying the bliss of emancipation. Sitting there he had fulfilled, after many years of effort and struggle, the entire course of the higher evolution of the individual. He had defeated the forces of Mara and was now a conqueror. He had dissolved all mental defilements, resolved all psychological conditionings. He had seen the Truth, seen Reality. He had not just had a glimpse of the truth but now saw it steadily, all the time, having fully absorbed and assimilated it. He was now an embodiment of the Truth, an embodiment of Reality. He was Reality in human form. He was a new kind of being: a New Man.

A question now arises: what happened next? The Buddha has gained Enlightenment—humanity now has a Buddha on its hands. What does humanity *do* with the

Buddha? And what does he do with himself?

At this point, something very mysterious happens. In a way that we cannot hope to understand, *Enlightenment begins to communicate itself.* In other words, the Buddha starts to communicate with other living beings: the New Man speaks. First of all, he simply speaks to himself; then he speaks to the gods; finally, he speaks to human beings.

As for what he says to himself, there are a number of different accounts of this first utterance, but they are substantially the same. According to the oldest Pali account, the Buddha speaks two verses—of which I must provide two different translations. Buddhadatta's prose translation offers the more or less exact meaning, while Sir Edwin Arnold's verse rendering gives a better impression of the spirit:

> 'Many a birth have I traversed in this round of lives and deaths, vainly seeking the builder of this house. Sorrowful is repeated birth. Oh house builder, you are seen. Never again shall you build the house. All your rafters are broken. Your ridge pole is shattered. My mind has gone to dissolution. I have attained the end of craving.'[*]

In Sir Edwin Arnold's much more vigorous version we find:

> 'Many a house of life
> Hath held me—seeking ever him who wrought
> These prisons of the senses, sorrow-fraught;
>   Sore was my ceaseless strife!
>   'But now,
> Thou Builder of this Tabernacle—Thou!
> I know Thee! Never shalt Thou build again

---

[*] *Dhammapada* 10, 8-9 (153-154) trans. Buddhadata

These walls of pain,
Nor raise the roof-tree of deceits, nor lay
      Fresh rafters on the clay;
Broken Thy house is, and the ridge-pole split!
      Delusion fashioned it!
Safe pass I thence—deliverance to obtain.'[*]

These two verses constitute what is technically known as
an *Udana*. The word *udana* means 'exhalation', 'a breathing
out'. It also means that which *is* breathed out—something
spoken under intense emotional pressure. Such utterances
are always in metrical form. The Buddha is saying, 'I'm
free, I've made it!' His six-year quest is complete. He has
broken through. Looking back into the past over hundreds
and thousands of lives and seeing where he had been going
wrong, where the mistakes and delusions lay, it is not
surprising that there should have been a tremendous up-
surge of energy and emotion.

Next, the Buddha speaks to the gods—or, rather, speaks
to Brahmasahampati, the 'Lord of a Thousand Worlds':

'Opened for those who hear are the doors of the
      Deathless, Brahma,
Let them give forth their faith;
Thinking of useless fatigue, Brahma, I have not
      preached *dhamma*
Sublime and excellent for men.'[**]

In order to understand this verse we have to refer back to
the episode in which it occurs. According to the scriptures,
after his Enlightenment the Buddha felt inclined to say
nothing about it to anyone. He realized that the truth he

---

[*] Sir Edwin Arnold *The Light of Asia*, Routledge and Kegan Paul,
      London, 1971, p.115
[**] *Majjhima Nikaya I (Middle Length Sayings)*, Ariyapariyesana Sutta,
trans. I.B. Horner, Pali Text Society, London, 1967, p. 213

had discovered went far beyond the capacities of the vast majority of people. He saw that people were immersed in craving and ignorance; they would not be able to understand the Truth even if he uttered it.

To Brahmasahampati, this was terrible. If the Buddha did not teach, he reflected, then the whole world would perish. It might progress materially, people might become prosperous and happy after a fashion, but there would be no *value* in it if the Buddha would not teach, if there were to be no spiritual element in their existence. So he appeared in front of the Buddha, like a great golden light, and begged him to make known to humanity the truth he had discovered. 'There are just a few', he said, 'whose eyes are covered with only a little dust. For their sake, teach the truth you have realized.'

At that, the Buddha looked out over the world with his eye of intuitive insight. He then saw all the beings who made up the mass of humanity to be like lotus flowers growing in a lake. The vast majority were sunk in the mud beneath the water, but some had grown up a little so as to touch the surface. Just a very few were even standing completely free of the water. Seeing this, he was overwhelmed with compassion and decided that he would teach. It was at that point that he finally addressed Brahma in the words already quoted: 'Open to them are the doors of the immortal': open to humanity, open to those with just a little dust on their eyes. 'Let them that have ears release their faith.'

One or two points here deserve comment. Firstly, the Buddha uses the term 'immortal'. In early Buddhist texts we do not find the expression *Nibbana*; more often we find the Pali term *amata* (Sanskrit *amrita*). This word means 'nectar of immortality', the deathless, something above and beyond the changes of the world, above and beyond time. It is a sort of synonym for Nibbana, or Enlightenment. The

Buddha has now attained Enlightenment; he has broken through into the Transcendental dimension of consciousness. Now others can follow his example and his teaching, they too can become Enlightened. The doors to the immortal are now open. Anybody who is prepared to make the effort may enter, anyone who is prepared to release their faith.

In the original Pali, the phrase 'release their faith' is rather ambiguous. It can mean *giving up*—releasing *wrong faith*, and it can also mean releasing—in the sense of developing—*right* faith.

Faith, *saddha* (Sanskrit *shraddha*), is of great importance in the Buddhist spiritual tradition. This kind of faith is not *blind belief*; in the Buddhist context, faith is the authentic, living, response of the whole being—especially the emotional part of our being—to something which we intuitively perceive to be greater, nobler, more sublime and more worthwhile than ourselves as we are now, something to which we feel we ought to dedicate ourselves, surrender ourselves, something for the sake of which we ought to *live*. Without faith in this sense there is no spiritual life, no development. Unfortunately, this kind of faith is rather lacking nowadays. There is plenty of faith in inferior values, but faith—in the sense of confidence in something higher than ourselves—is comparatively rare.

Finally, the Buddha speaks to human beings. He decides to teach. But *who* is he to teach? Who will be first? Who will learn the doctrine most quickly?

At first the Buddha thought of his first teacher, Alara the Kalama, a very good and noble man—but one who had not been able to lead him to the highest truth because he had not himself realized it. We are told, however, that a god appeared to tell the Buddha that Alara the Kalama had died, just a week beforehand. So the Buddha then thought of his second teacher, Udaka Ramaputta, under whom he had also learned many useful things. He then became aware that Udaka Ramaputta too had died, only the previous evening. Finally, he thought of the five ascetics, his five disciple-companions from the days when he had practised self-mortification. They had stayed with him and looked after him when he was practising those terrible austerities in the hope that they would be able to benefit from his eventual realization. When the Buddha had realized that self-mortification was not the way, and had started taking solid food, they had left him in disgust. But now he thought of them: 'Let me teach the Dhamma first of all to these five.'

At that time they were living just a few miles out of Benares, in the Deer Park at Isipatana. So the Buddha left Buddhagaya (which was then known as Uruvela), and set off to walk the hundred miles to Benares.

He had not been on the road for very long when he met an ascetic belonging to a sect known as the Ajivakas. His name was Upaka. When from a distance Upaka saw the Buddha coming, he was very impressed by his appearance. The Buddha had gained Enlightenment only seven weeks beforehand. He was bright, shining, cheerful and happy. As they drew near, they stopped and greeted each other. As is the custom in India, even to this day, Upaka asked two questions: 'Who is your teacher?' and 'Which doctrine do you profess?'

Upaka got rather more than he bargained for, for the Buddha replied in four resounding verses—his first utterance to humanity:

'Victorious over all, Omniscient am I
Among all things undefiled,
Leaving all, through death of craving freed,
By knowing myself, whom should I point to?

'For me there is no teacher,
One like me does not exist,
In the world with its *devas*
No one equals me.

For I am perfected in the world,
A teacher supreme am I,
I alone am all-awakened,
Become cool am I, Nibbana-attained.

To turn the *dhamma*-wheel
I go to Kasi's city,
Beating the drum of deathlessness
In a world that's blind become.'*

What we cannot fail to notice here, once we've recovered from the shock, is the Buddha's complete self-confidence—a self-confidence that was to last for the rest of his life. There is no false humility, and no false pride either. He makes a simple statement of fact because he knows exactly what has happened, who he is, and what he is going to do. He knows that he has gained Enlightenment; he knows that he is free; he knows that he is a New Man—in that there is as yet no one else like him anywhere in the world; and he knows that he is going to teach.

As if to check that he has heard correctly, Upaka points out that he seems to be claiming to be a *Jina*, a conqueror, a Buddha. The Buddha confirms this in another resounding verse:

'Like me, they are victors indeed
Who have won destruction of the cankers [*asavas*];
Vanquished by me are evil things,

---

* *Majjhima Nikaya I (Middle Length Sayings)*, Ariyapariyesana Sutta, trans. I.B. Horner, Pali Text Society, London, 1967, p. 214–5

Therefore am I, Upaka, a victor.'*

Upaka thinks for a moment, and simply says 'Maybe'. Shaking his head, he goes off, we are told, by a by-path.

This incident is very significant. We ourselves are rather like Upaka. We too are confronted, as it were, by the figure of the Buddha, and by his teaching. We too take a look at the Buddha, and listen to the Dhamma for a while. Then, just like Upaka, we say, 'Maybe there is something in it.' But then we shake our heads and go off on some little by-path of our own. In this way we miss a great opportunity, perhaps forever.

The Buddha then proceeded to Benares, to the Deer Park at Isipatana, arriving on a full moon day. This was a beautiful coincidence. He had been walking for a week, and now, on the full moon day exactly two lunar months after his Enlightenment, he arrived at the Deer Park at Isipatana. The five ascetics were there; apparently they had been living there for some time. When they saw the Buddha coming they started to speak among themselves: 'Look, there is that fellow Gautama, the one who gave up, the one who started living luxuriously and taking solid food. He has had the nerve to come back! All right, let him come! If he wants, he even can sit with us for a while, but let's not show him any respect at all.'

As the Buddha came nearer, the five ascetics tried to take no notice. But when he drew close they simply could not help themselves. They rose like humble pupils and moved forward. One politely took his bowl while another took the spare robe he was carrying; another prepared a seat while another brought some water for the Buddha to wash his feet. However, even though they could not help showing respect, they still addressed him by his personal name,

---

* *Majjhima Nikaya I (Middle Length Sayings)*, Ariyapariyesana Sutta, trans. I.B. Horner, Pali Text Society, London, 1967, p. 215

Gautama, and addressed him also as *avuso*, which is a familiar mode of address among monks, meaning 'friend'. In response, the Buddha simply said, 'Do not address me in this way, this is not proper, not appropriate. I am no longer just your friend. I have gained Enlightenment. I teach the Dhamma. If you practise according to my teaching you too will gain Enlightenment.'

The five ascetics did not believe him. They could not take him seriously. 'Look here,' they said, 'For all those years you practised self-mortification. You went beyond what anybody else has done in this life. But you did not gain Enlightenment. Now you've gone back to a comfortable, easy, way of living. How do you think you can gain Enlightenment by that means?'

Again the Buddha insisted: 'No. I *am* the Enlightened One. If you follow my teaching you too will become Enlightened.'

They still could not accept what the Buddha was saying. Three times the Buddha therefore made his declaration, and three times they refused to accept his claim. Then he said: 'Look, in all the time that you knew me before, did I ever speak in this way? Have I ever been so certain, so emphatic? Have I ever claimed before that I have gained Enlightenment?' They conceded that he had not. 'All right. Now let me teach you.' In this way he began to convince them, and they became at least open-minded about what he was saying.

The *sutta* describes what happened next very beautifully. Apparently, the Buddha started teaching the ascetics in turns. While two of them remained listening to the Buddha in the Deer Park, the other three would go out for alms, collecting food from house to house. What the three of them collected, all six would eat. Then the Buddha would teach those three, while the two others went out for alms. So far as we can tell, the six of them lived in this way throughout the rainy season, for twelve or more weeks, taking it in turns to collect food and to receive instruction from the Buddha. At the end of that period, we are told, all five gained Enlightenment. They too became 'New Men'. There were now six New Men in the world.

There is a very important point to be noted here. So far I have been following the oldest account—from the *Majjhima Nikaya*. While this account tells us the way in which the Buddha taught the five ascetics, and tells us that the five ascetics became Enlightened, the *sutta* does not actually tell us *what* the Buddha taught them. We simply do not know what teaching he gave. That remains a mystery.

Later accounts, even in the Pali Canon, try to fill in the blank, especially with a text known as the *Dhammacakkappavattana Sutta*—the *sutta*, or discourse, on the 'setting in motion of the Wheel of the Doctrine'. This is a useful—if rather stereotyped—summary of the Buddha's teaching which deals with the doctrines of the Middle Way, the Four Noble Truths, and the Noble Eightfold Path. It is quite possible that it represents the substance of a talk actually given by the Buddha on some occasion. But it is important to remember that the *earliest* account of the 'conversion' of those five ascetics makes no mention of any particular teaching at all.

Although some will find this lack of detailed information very unsatisfactory, I personally find it very suggestive. It changes the nature of the whole episode. The Buddha taught the five ascetics; but he teaches *anyone*. He taught *then*, but he teaches *now*. This means that the teaching cannot ever be reduced to a specific formula or set of doctrines. You can never say that you have all of the Buddha's teaching under your thumb, all written down: 'If I learn this and study that, I will *have* Buddhism, *have* the Buddha's teaching.' The teaching is not any specific doctrine. The teaching, as the Buddha himself was to say on another occasion, is whatever conduces to Enlightenment, whatever helps you to grow, whatever helps you to develop.

This is brought out very clearly in a later, Mahayana sutra, the *Diamond Sutra*. Here, the monk Subhuti, speaking under the Buddha's inspiration, says:

> 'The Tathagata [the Buddha] has no formulated teaching to enunciate. Wherefore? Because the Tathagata has said that Truth is uncontainable and inexpressible. It neither is nor is it not.—
>
> Thus it is that this unformulated Principle is the foundation of the different systems of all the sages.'[*]

This is only a step away from saying that the Buddha does not actually speak at all, that the New Man remains silent. Another great Mahayana sutra, the *Lankavatara Sutra*, actually takes this step. The Buddha says here,

> 'From the night of the Enlightenment to the night of the Tathagata's Parinirvana [passing away], he has not uttered, nor ever will he utter, one word.'[**]

In other words, the Buddha has not said anything which can be *identified* as the teaching.

For this reason we can never pin the Buddha's teaching down to any simple formula, to the 'three of this' or the 'four of that', or to any such set of principles. Really, the teaching is nothing verbal, nothing conceptual, at all. The teaching is a realization and an *influence*. It is a communication between the Enlightened and the unenlightened. Certainly, it sometimes makes *use* of words, doctrines, and so on, but it can never be reduced to them.

---

[*] *Diamond Sutra* trans. A.F. Price, Buddhist Society, London 1947, p.32

[**] D. Goddard (ed.), *A Buddhist Bible*, Beacon Press, Boston, 1970, p.348

All this rather alters our picture of what happened in the Deer Park at Isipatana. We may tend to imagine the Buddha arriving at the Deer Park, taking out his notes, and giving a lecture to the five ascetics—at the end of which they become Enlightened—then going off to give his lecture somewhere else. Traditional Buddhist art reinforces this view. In traditional works the Buddha is usually depicted sitting cross-legged on a magnificent, ornately decorated, throne, the five ascetics kneeling submissively at his feet while he preaches. But, as we have seen, the Buddha had great difficulty in getting the five ascetics even to listen to him. He certainly did not deliver a formal address, much less still a lecture. He thrashed things out with them, in personal discussion, over a period of weeks and months.

So on the occasion of Dhamma Day we do not celebrate the Dhamma in the sense of any particular rigid formulation of the Truth, any particular text or scripture—however useful, however ancient, or however inspiring. What we celebrate is the first impact of the Enlightened Man on the unenlightened, the first impact of the New Man on the old men. This impact finds expression in terms of speech, but it is not confined to speech. Today we are celebrating the impact of the New Man on the 'old men' and 'old women' of the *present generation*: upon *ourselves*.

Life today is a complicated and sometimes difficult business. It is full of distractions, as though there are lots of clutching fingers trying to get at us, trying to take hold of us, all the time. Under such conditions it is only too easy to forget what is really the main purpose of human existence. It is only too easy to ignore, or forget, the possibility of developing oneself, of growing in the direction of Enlightenment. Occasions such as this festival help us to remember.

There are many ways in which we can grow and

develop. We can grow with the help of meditation, with the help of philosophizing—as an activity of the mind; we can grow with the help of the practice of the arts, and so on. As this process unfolds we will sooner or later find ourselves in contact with others who are also growing, also developing. As we weave a network of relationships with these people, coming subtley more and more in contact with one another, we shall one day wake up to the fact that we collectively form a spiritual community, united by common ideals and a common way of life. If, as a result of the impact of the New Man on our lives, we ourselves start becoming 'new men' and 'new women', evolving together and forming a new spiritual community, then the New Man will not have spoken in vain.

A Wreath of Blue Lotus

Because there is really only one Going for Refuge, there can really only be one kind of 'ordination'. But ordination may take place in a number of ways. Historically speaking, as we can see from the Pali scriptures, it could take place when the Buddha, upon meeting and communicating with someone, saw that the person was ready to go for Refuge, ready to commit himself. On such an occasion, the Buddha would simply say, 'Come, O monk! *(Ehi bhikhkave!)* Lead the spiritual life *(brahmachariya)* for the destruction of suffering.' And the person was ordained. It could be as simple as that. Similarly, we find that ordination could take place when someone, deeply impressed by the Buddha's teaching, repeated the formula: 'To the Buddha for Refuge I go. To the Dhamma for Refuge I go. To the Sangha for Refuge I go,'—and the Buddha accepted that. Otherwise, the ordination could take place when the individual concerned was 'accepted' by an assembly of five or ten monks. However, the episode with which we shall be concerned here centres upon a rather unusual—in fact a quite unique— form of ordination.

At one time the Buddha was staying among the Shakyas of Kapilavastu in a park known as the Banyan Park. The Shakyans were the people among whom the Buddha was born, and among whom he grew up. Kapilavastu was their capital. After the Buddha's Enlightenment many Shakyans became his followers; in particular, many young Shakyan men left home and became 'monks' under his guidance. Among these was of course Ananda, the Buddha's constant companion in his later years.

While the Buddha was staying at Kapilavastu many people came to see him—including friends and relations he had known before. Among these came Mahaprajapati, the Buddha's maternal aunt and foster-mother. (The Buddha's own mother, Mayadevi, had died when he was only a few days old, and it was Mahaprajapati who had brought him up.)

On this occasion Mahaprajapati came with an unusual—even unprecedented—request. This was nothing less than that women should be permitted to go forth from home into the homeless life under the Dhamma Vinaya set forth by the Buddha. She wanted to be ordained.

The Buddha's response was a categorical refusal. There was no beating about the bush: he just said no. Three times Mahaprajapati made her request and three times the Buddha refused. In fact he asked her not even to wish for such a thing, and, in the end, she just had to go away unsatisfied. The translation of the Pali text tells us, moreover, that she went away 'sad, sorrowful, tearful, and wailing'.

The second half of the episode takes place some time later. We are not told exactly when it takes place, but it is clear that the Buddha has left Kapilavastu. He has been wandering from place to place and has now come to Vaisali and is staying in the Mahavana, the 'great grove', or 'great forest', at the 'Hall of the Peaked Gable'. Meanwhile, Mahaprajapati has not been idle. She has not accepted the Buddha's refusal to allow women to be ordained and proceeds to get her hair cut off, dons saffron robes, and sets off for Vaisali with a number of Shakyan women. She is clearly a very determined lady; she won't take no for an answer, even from the Buddha.

Eventually she arrives at the Hall of the Peaked Gable and takes her stand outside the porch. Her feet are of course swollen and dust begrimed after the long journey, and we are told that she is sad, sorrowful, weeping and wailing.

Sooner or later Ananda finds her. He knows her, of course, because he is also a kinsman of the Buddha and therefore her kinsman too. He asks her what she wants and why she is so upset, and she replies that she is upset because the Buddha will not permit women to Go Forth from home into the homeless life.

Ananda is a very sympathetic soul. He feels sorry for Mahaprajapati and does his best to help. He goes immediately to see the Buddha, saying that Mahaprajapati has come all the way from Kapilavastu and is now standing outside the porch weeping and wailing. He also suggests, out of the kindness of his heart, that the Buddha should grant her request.

But the Buddha refuses Ananda's request just as categorically as he had refused Mahaprajapati's, and asks him not to wish for any such thing. Three times Ananda makes his request, and three times the Buddha refuses. However, Ananda does not give up. After all, he knows the Buddha very well, and so argues with him, saying, 'Suppose women *were* to Go Forth from home into the homeless life under the Dhamma Vinaya set forth by the Tathagata, would they be capable of attaining the fruits of Stream Entry, or the Fruit of Once Returning, or the Fruit of Never Returning, or the Fruit of Arahantship?'

When the Buddha admits that women are so capable, Ananda seizes his opportunity. He reminds the Buddha that Mahaprajapati was of great service to the Buddha when he was an infant; on the death of his mother she actually suckled him. It would therefore be a good thing, he says, if women were permitted to Go Forth from home into the homeless life. The Buddha is unable to resist this argument, and grants Mahaprajapati's request.

He grants it, however, on certain conditions. He tells Ananda that if Mahaprajapati will undertake to keep eight important rules, then that will be reckoned as full ordination. The rules are as follows:

A sister, even if she be an hundred years in the robes, shall salute, shall rise up before, shall bow down before, shall perform all duties of respect unto a brother—even if that brother have only just taken the robes. Let this rule never be broken, but be honoured, esteemed, reverenced, and observed as long as life doth last.

Secondly, a sister shall not spend the rainy season in a district where there is no brother residing. Let this rule never be broken....

Thirdly, at the half month let a sister await two things from the Order of Brethren, namely the appointing of the Sabbath [this is the translator's rather strange word for the *uposatha*] and the coming of a brother to preach the sermon. Let this rule never be broken....

Fourthly, at the end of keeping the rainy season let a sister, in presence of both Orders, of Brethren and of Sisters, invite enquiry in respect of three things, namely, of things seen, heard, and suspected. Let this rule never be broken....

Fifthly, a sister guilty of serious wrong-doing shall do penance for the half-month to both Orders. Let this rule never be broken....

Sixthly, when a sister has passed two seasons in the practice of the Six Rules she may ask for full orders from both Orders. Let this rule never be broken....

Seventhly, a sister shall not in any case abuse or censure a brother. Let this rule never be broken....

Eighthly, henceforth is forbidden the right of a sister to have speech among brethren, but not forbidden is the speaking of brethren unto sisters. Let this rule never be broken, but be honoured, esteemed, reverenced, and observed as long as life doth last.[*]

On hearing this reply, Ananda goes to Mahaprajapati and tells her what the Buddha has said. This is her response:

'Just as, lord Ananda, a woman or a man, youthful, of tender age, fond of self-adornment, having washed the head and having gotten a wreath of blue lotus or of jasmine or of scented-creeper flowers, should take it with both hands and place it atop of the head,—even so do I, lord Ananda, take upon me these Eight Important Rules, never to be broken so long as life doth last.'[**]

Ananda now returns to the Buddha and tells him that Mahaprajapati has accepted the eight rules and is therefore now fully ordained.

This, then, is the episode with which we are concerned. This is our wreath of blue lotus. Clearly, it provides us with a good deal of material for reflection. I am going to concentrate on just one important part: the eight important rules. Why did they take the particular form that they did? And what are we to make of Mahaprajapati's response to them?

Before looking at the rules, however, we must briefly examine Mahaprajapati's behaviour after the Buddha's initial refusal. As we have seen, she gets her hair cut off, dons the saffron robes, and sets off for Vaisali with a number of Shakyan women. Finally, she stands outside the porch of the Hall of the Peaked Gable. In doing all this, she seems to be trying to force the Buddha's hand. We might even say that she is trying to present the Buddha with a *fait accompli*. After all, she has left home, shaved her head, and

---

[*]
[**]Vinaya Pitaka, ii, 10, quoted in *Some Sayings of the Buddha*, pp. 121–2
  Ibid p.123

donned the saffron robes. She is in effect now a nun, so the Buddha might as well accept the situation, might as well permit her to do what she has in fact already done.

Now the *fait accompli* is a very interesting phenomenon. Essentially, a *fait accompli* consists in creating a situation in which the other person is, in effect, deprived of their power of choice or decision. I say *in effect* because they are not literally deprived of it; nevertheless, a situation is created in which they can exercise that power only at the cost of a great deal of trouble and even a great deal of unpleasantness. The *fait accompli* involves an element of what we may describe as emotional blackmail, and is thus a form of coercion. This of course means that it is a form of violence, and is hence completely out of place in the spiritual life. If you present someone with a *fait accompli* you are not treating them as an individual. But this is what Mahaprajapati did: she tried to force the Buddha's hand. Her desire to Go Forth was no doubt sincere but, in this connection, she did not treat the Buddha with very much respect.

We are also told that she stood outside the porch 'sad, sorrowful, weeping and wailing'. One can perhaps understand her being sad and sorrowful, but what about the weeping and wailing? It would seem that she was trying to get her way in a rather childish fashion. We can contrast this with Ananda's attitude. Ananda argued with the Buddha. He prepared his ground and gave reasons as to why women should be permitted to Go Forth—with the result that the Buddha was unable to resist his request; he was unable to resist reason, unable to resist argument.

This part of the episode is surely of some significance. The *fait accompli* in fact failed—as it always does in the long run. Emotional blackmail fails, attempted coercion fails. On the other hand, reason suffused with sympathy succeeds. Mahaprajapati herself failed to gain her point, but Ananda gained it for her.

It is now time that we moved on to the eight important rules themselves. Why did they take the particular form they did?

Perhaps the first thing that strikes us about them is that they are quite severe, even quite harsh. We cannot quite help feeling that the Buddha is perhaps being rather unfair towards Mahaprajapati—though he no doubt knew her better than we do. Indeed, the Buddha seems to be being quite unjust to women in general. The eight important rules would certainly make the blood of a modern feminist boil with rage, and they might even make some men a little uneasy. Let's go into the matter a little.

If we look at these rules, it is rather obvious that their main function is to subordinate the order of nuns to the order of monks, to make the *bhikkhunis* completely dependent on the *bhikkhus*. The *bhikkhunis*, the nuns, are to be kept in a state of perpetual pupilage. What could have been the reason for this?

One scholar has suggested that Mahaprajapati's request created an 'organizational problem' for the Buddha (it seems that even the Buddha had organizational problems!). By this time the order of monks had been in existence for about twenty years. Organizationally speaking, the Buddha was faced with three alternatives. He could admit women to the existing order of monks, thus creating a single unified order, he could create an entirely separate and independent order for women, or he could subordinate the order of nuns to the order of monks.

The first of these options was clearly out of the question. Both monks and nuns were expected to lead lives of celibacy and this would presumably have been rather difficult if they were living together as members of a single unified order. The second alternative was out of the question too. The Buddha could hardly be the head of two quite separate, independent, orders. In any case, he was—

externally at least—a man, and a man could hardly be the head of an order of nuns. If it was really to be separate and independent, that order of nuns would have to be headed by a woman. That left only the third alternative, that of subordinating the order of nuns to the order of monks. This, according to the scholar, is the alternative that the Buddha adopted.

This explanation is certainly of interest. There may even be some truth in it. But it does not really suffice to explain the specific form in which the eight important rules were presented. Something more than organizational convenience seems to have been involved. Perhaps it would help if we tried to understand what it was that the rules were intended to prevent. To do this, however, we have to look at rules in general.

If we look at the *Vinaya-Pitaka*, or 'The Book of the Discipline', we find that it contains many rules, of many different kinds. There are rules for monks, and rules for nuns. According to the Theravada tradition, there are, altogether, two-hundred-and-twenty-seven rules for monks, and three-hundred-and-eleven rules for nuns. How did these rules come to be laid down?

It is certain that the Buddha did not draw them all up in advance. He did not sit down under his Bodhi tree and think, 'What sort of Sangha would I like to have? And what sort of rules should it observe? How should it be constituted?' The Buddha laid down rules in response to unskilful behaviour on the part of a member, or members, of the Sangha. So long as there was no unskilful behaviour there were no rules; the Buddha was not interested in laying down rules for their own sake. He was interested simply in the moral and spiritual development of the individual, and laid down rules only when 'forced' to do so.

These eight important rules, however, *were* laid down in advance of any offence actually committed by

Mahaprajapati. But the same principle does perhaps apply.

The effect of these rules is to subordinate the order of nuns to the order of monks. It is to make the *bhikkhunis* completely dependent, organizationally speaking, on the *bhikkhus*. So what kind of unskilful behaviour are the eight rules meant to prevent? To what kind of possible offences do they refer?

Clearly they are meant to prevent the nuns claiming equality with, or superiority over, monks. That is to say, they are meant to prevent women claiming equality with, or superiority over, men. In other words, we could say that they are meant to prevent an irruption of *feminism* into the order.

To say this does not mean that the Buddha did not believe in equal rights for women in the ordinary social sense. It does not mean that he did not believe that a woman could be spiritually superior to a man. After all, he had told Ananda quite categorically that women were capable of attaining the fruits of Stream Entry and so on, and, presumably, a woman who was a Stream Entrant was spiritually superior to a man who was still a worldling. So what the Buddha wanted to do, it seems, was to prevent women from Going Forth *for the wrong reasons*, that is, for social rather than for purely spiritual reasons.

There are indications that this sort of thing did sometimes happen afterwards, despite the Buddha's precautions. A woman might seek ordination because she wanted to be free from her husband, or because she was a widow and wanted to be more highly respected—which as a nun she would be—or because her parents were unable or unwilling to find her a husband. The same sort of thing can happen even in modern times.

I received my *shramanera* ordination from U Chandramani Mahathera at Kusinara. U Chandramani—fortunately for me—was very generous with his ordinations. Amongst others, he ordained a large number of women. He did not ordain them as *shramaneris,* since that was no longer possible, but as *anagarikas.* Eventually he ordained so many women that he was begged to stop by his *bhikkhu* disciples. The women whom he had ordained were mostly Nepalese and, as I knew from my personal contact with them, they wanted ordination mainly for social reasons. They wanted to enjoy the same rights as men, and saw ordination as a means of achieving this end. In most cases they were not really interested in the spiritual life at all.

This seems to have been the sort of situation that the Buddha wanted to prevent, and this is why he set forth the eight important rules. He was trying to make quite sure that Mahaprajapati wanted to Go Forth for purely spiritual reasons, that she really wanted to go for Refuge, really wanted to gain Enlightenment.

We can take things even further than this. We have seen that Mahaprajapati tried to present the Buddha with a *fait accompli.* And we have seen that she tried to get her own way in a rather childish fashion. In Mahaprajapati, there was a strong element of what William Blake called the 'Female Will'. In fact, from a certain point of view, she was almost an embodiment of that Female Will. The Buddha saw that before Mahaprajapati could truly Go Forth the Female Will had to annihilated—and the eight important rules were intended to do just that. At this point I should perhaps say a few words about what Blake meant by the Female Will.

According to Blake, in the 'unfallen Individual', reason and emotion, 'masculine' and 'feminine', are united. The feminine 'portion' of the fundamentally bisexual Individual is called the 'Emanation'. With the Fall of Man—to summarize rather rapidly—Reason and Emotion are divided: the Emanation is divided from the Individual and takes the Female form, and Man is left as what Blake calls a 'Dark Spectre'. Worse still, the Emanation acquires a will of her own and this 'Female Will' acts in opposition to her consort. As S. Foster Damon puts it, 'The Emanation's self-centred pride seeks dominion over the male. She is jealous of all his activities, and seeks to stop them by denying her husband his freedom.... She is even jealous of her husband's labours, which take his attention from her; so she prevents his working.'*

It is this kind of spirit, it seems, that the Buddha wanted to prevent from entering the Sangha, he wanted to curb the Female Will, and this is why he set forth the eight important rules.

How then does Mahaprajapati receive the rules? She says:

'Just as, lord Ananda, a woman or a man, youthful, of tender age, fond of self-adornment, having washed the head and having gotten a wreath of blue lotus or of jasmine or of scented-creeper flowers, should take it with both hands and place it atop of the head,—even so do I, lord Ananda, take upon me these Eight Important Rules, never to be broken so long as life doth last.'

From these words it is clear that Mahaprajapati accepts the eight important rules in a completely positive spirit. She passes the test—if it is a test—and the Female Will is annihilated in her. She really did want to Go Forth, really did want to gain Enlightenment. And gain Enlightenment she eventually did.

In the *Therigatha*, or the 'Verses of the Elder Nuns', there are some very interesting verses attributed to Mahaprajapati after her attainment of Enlightenment:

---

* S. Foster Damon, *A Blake Dictionary*, London 1979, p.121

'(157)Buddha, Hero, homage to you, O best of all crea-
tures, who released me and many other people from
pain. (158)All pain is known; craving as the cause is
dried up; the Noble Eightfold Way has been
developed; cessation has been attained by me.
(159)Formerly I was mother, son, father, brother, and
grandmother; not having proper knowledge I jour-
neyed on without expiation. (160)That blessed one has
indeed been seen by me; this is the last body; journey-
ing on from rebirth to rebirth has been completely
eliminated; there is now no renewed existence. (161)I
see the disciples all together putting forth energy,
resolute, always with strong effort; this is homage to
the Buddhas. (162)Truly for the sake of many Maya
bore Gotama. She thrust away the mass of pain of
those struck by sickness and death.'[*]

The last verse but one is particularly beautiful.
Mahaprajapati says, 'I see the disciples all together putting
forth energy, resolute, always with strong effort; this is
homage to the Buddhas.' We might say that this verse
could serve as a motto for the entire Sangha—past, present,
and future. We could also say that Mahaprajapati's accep-
tance of the eight important rules and her attainment of
Enlightenment are by no means unconnected. The eight
important rules made sure that her Going Forth was sincere; they made sure that she really wanted to be ordained,
really wanted to go for Refuge. They made sure that her
motivation was not social but spiritual. The eight important rules are like a great blazing fire, a fire in which all the
impurities in Mahaprajapati's wish for ordination were
burned up, were consumed, and from that fire
Mahaprajapati emerged triumphant. To her, the eight

---

[*] *The Elders' Verses II (Therigatha)*, trans. K.R. Norman, Luzac & Co.,
London 1971, p.18

important rules were not a crown of thorns but a 'wreath of blue lotus'. They were not something to be endured, but something to be enjoyed. I am reminded in this connection of a passage in the *Diamond Sutra*:

'Moreover, Subhuti, the spot of earth where this Sutra will be revealed, that spot of earth will be worthy of worship by the whole world with its Gods, men and Asuras, worthy of being saluted respectfully, worthy of being honoured by circumambulation,—like a shrine will be that spot of earth. And yet Subhuti, those sons and daughters of good family, who will take up these very Sutras, and will bear them in mind, recite and study them, they will be humbled,—well humbled will they be! And why? The impure deeds which these beings have done in their former lives, and which are liable to lead them into states of woe,— in this very life they will, by means of that humiliation, annul those impure deeds of their former lives, and they will reach the enlightenment of a Buddha.'[*]

Before concluding, I would like to generalize a little from the episode with which we have been concerned. I have spoken of the Buddha wanting to be quite sure that Mahaprajapati wanted to Go Forth for purely spiritual reasons. But this should not be seen as applying only to Mahaprajapati, or even only to women. It applies to *all* who want to Go Forth, to all who want to go for Refuge, to all who want to be ordained.

It is important that one should want to do the right thing for the right reason. Indeed, in the sphere of spiritual life, the right thing is not the right thing *unless* one does it for the right reason. In principle, the eight important rules

---

[*] E. Conze, *Buddhist Wisdom Books*, George Allen & Unwin, London, 1958, p.56

represent all those factors that prevent us from Going Forth until we are really ready to do so. To begin with, of course, we may experience those factors not as a wreath of blue lotus, but indeed as a crown of thorns. We may feel very ill-used, very hard done by; we may go around wearing a martyred look. We may even feel angry and resentful that we are not being ordained. But a time comes when we no longer experience the crown of thorns as a crown of thorns but as a wreath of blue lotus. We accept that we are not ready for ordination. Then, paradoxically, we find—or it is found—that we *are* ready.

At this point a question may arise. Must our desire for ordination be perfectly pure before we can be ordained? In the case of Mahaprajapati this seems to have been what the Buddha insisted upon—perfect purity of motive at least with regard to what Blake called the Female Will. In modern times, when life is so much more complicated than it was in the Buddha's day, one might say that we cannot expect the desire for ordination always to be perfectly pure. But, at the same time, we can *expect* it to be so, in the sense that we must be prepared to put as much of our energy as we possibly can into the task of spiritual self-development, into the Going for Refuge. Not only that, we must be prepared to take active steps to *put* all our energies into it. If we can do that then we are ready to Go Forth, ready to go for Refuge.

There is one thing, however, that we must remember. So far as most people are concerned, the Going for Refuge is—to begin with—an 'effective' rather than a 'real' Going for Refuge.* Inasmuch as it is only an effective Going for Refuge, we can fall away from it. It is therefore not only

---

* The Going for Refuge is 'effective' when insight into, and commitment to, the spiritual path is sufficiently deep and sufficiently sincere to serve as a strong basis for continued striving. 'Real' Going for Refuge coincides with Stream Entry. From this Going for Refuge one cannot fall away. See Sangharakshita, *Going for Refuge*, Windhorse, Glasgow 1983

necessary to make sure that our desire for ordination is pure, but to make sure that we *keep* it pure. It is also necessary to make sure that our motive for being in the order remains pure after ordination. We do this by remaining aware and mindful, by remaining emotionally positive, by living and working under conditions which are conducive to our spiritual development, by keeping in close touch with our spiritual friends, and by coming together repeatedly and in large numbers. Otherwise, we may fall by the wayside.

There is just one more point to be made. The eight important rules ensured that Mahaprajapati's Going Forth was sincere. But Going for Refuge is an on-going process. It is not something that we do once and for all. Consequently we all need something like the eight important rules all the time, something that will make sure that our Going for Refuge really is a process that is constantly deepening.

This something is not so difficult to find. We can find it in the positive critical feedback of our spiritual friends—in what has been called 'fierce friendship'. If we are to continue to develop spiritually, if we are to continue to deepen our Going for Refuge, then we will need genuine criticism. I am not of course suggesting that we need nothing *but* criticism—that can be counterproductive: we also need encouragement, appreciation, and inspiration. But we shall upon occasion certainly need criticism too. We shall need criticism that comes from the heart, criticism that is based upon positive emotion, on *metta*, criticism that is concerned only with our welfare, only with our development.

When we are given that criticism, how shall we receive it? Hopefully we will receive it in the same spirit that Mahaprajapati received the eight important rules from the Buddha: not as a crown of thorns, sharp and uncomfortable, but as a wreath of blue lotus resting beautifully on the top of our heads.

A Case of Dysentery

I am aware that the title of this talk is not like any of my previous titles. It is something of a change from the 'spiritual this', and the 'transcendental that', or the 'creative something else'. Perhaps it will raise a few eyebrows. Perhaps people will think that there has been a dreadful printing mistake or a deplorable lapse of good taste. Others might think that the title is meant to be symbolic or mythic. But there is nothing symbolic about it at all. My theme really is a case of dysentery—in the literal sense.

This is no ordinary case of dysentery, however. This particular case of dysentery is quite an important one, though not from a medical point of view. The case in question took place some two-thousand-five-hundred years ago, and we know about it because it is mentioned in the *Vinaya Pitaka* of the Theravada Pali Canon:

> Now at that time a certain brother was suffering from dysentery and lay where he had fallen down in his own excrements.
>
> And the Exalted One was going His rounds of the lodgings, with the venerable Ananda in attendance, and came to the lodging of that brother.
>
> Now the Exalted One saw that brother lying where he had fallen in his own excrements, and seeing him He went towards him, came to him, and said: 'Brother, what ails you?'
>
> 'I have dysentery, Lord.'
>
> 'But is there anyone taking care of you, brother?'

'No, Lord.'

'Why is it, brother, that the brethren do not take care of you?'

'I am useless to the brethren, Lord: therefore the brethren do not care for me.'

Then the Exalted One said to the venerable Ananda: 'Go you, Ananda, and fetch water. We will wash this brother.'

'Yes, Lord,' replied the venerable Ananda to the Exalted One. When he had fetched the water, the Exalted One poured it out, while the venerable Ananda washed that brother all over. Then the Exalted One taking him by the head and the venerable Ananda taking him by the feet, together they laid him on the bed.

Then the Exalted One, in this connexion and on this occasion, gathered the Order of Brethren together, and questioned the brethren, saying:

'Brethren, is there in such and such a lodging a brother who is sick?'

'There is, Lord.'

'And what ails that brother?'

'Lord, that brother has dysentery.'

'But, brethren, is there anyone taking care of him?'

'No, Lord.'

'Why not? Why do not the brethren take care of him?'

'That brother is useless to the brethren, Lord. That is why the brethren do not take care of him.'

'Brethren, ye have no mother and no father to take care of you. If ye will not take care of each other, who else, I ask, will do so? Brethren, he who would wait on me, let him wait on the sick.

If he have a teacher, let his teacher take care of him, so long as he is alive, and wait for his recovery. If he have a tutor or a lodger, a disciple or a fellow-lodger or a fellow-disciple, such should take care of him and await his recovery. If no one take care of him, it shall be reckoned an offence.'*

This passage deals with a significant episode in the collective life of the early Buddhist spiritual community. And, as I am sure you have realized, it deals with the kind of situation which might arise in the collective life of our own order, two-thousand-five-hundred years later, despite the lapse of time and despite the vast cultural differences. In this episode we are able to see how the Buddha responded to a situation of this sort, what advice he gave, what action he took, and so on. The episode is concerned with much more than the treatment of a sick monk; it is concerned with a number of principles of fundamental importance—some of them only *apparently* peripheral to the main issue.

The passage begins rather dramatically:

Now at that time a certain brother was suffering from dysentery and lay where he had fallen down in his own excrements.

This is a dreadful picture! Here is a brother, a *bhikkhu*—we are not told whether he is old or young, we are not even given his name—who is suffering from dysentery. It must be a really serious attack because he has fallen to the ground and is lying in his own excrement. Apparently he is too weak to get up. And he is on his own. There is nobody near, nobody within call, no one to help, no one to give him a drink of water. His condition is very pitiable.

The Exalted One was going His rounds of the lodgings, with the venerable Ananda in attendance, and came to the lodging of that brother.

---

* *Some Sayings of the Buddha* p.126–8

There are two points to notice here. The Buddha was going his rounds of the lodgings, and Ananda was in attendance. Ananda was the Buddha's cousin. He had known the Buddha—and the Buddha had known him—all his life. They had played together as boys, they had fought together, they had tumbled about together in the dust, they had practised archery together, and, years later, after the Buddha had gained Enlightenment, Ananda too went forth from home into the homeless life. He became a disciple of the Buddha and advanced steadily on the spiritual path. We know further that Ananda was the Buddha's constant companion for the last twenty years of his life. Ananda is usually described as the Buddha's 'attendant'. But why should the Buddha have needed a personal attendant?

The traditional explanations do not seem very adequate. It is simply suggested that the Buddha needed someone to wash his robe, arrange his interviews, and carry messages for him. Ananda did indeed do all these things, as well as many others. It is also said by the tradition that it was simply the 'custom' for a Buddha to have a personal attendant. Buddhas had always had personal attendants, and that was that—just as they had always had a particular tree under which they gained Enlightenment, or a particular horse, or a particular charioteer, or two particular chief disciples, and so on. Thus Ananda was the personal attendant of Gautama the Buddha. This is the traditional explanation; but it is not good enough, it does not go deep enough.

Ananda was not the first of these so-called personal attendants. There was, for example, Meghiya, whom we encounter in the *Udana*. Meghiya was the Buddha's personal attendant for a while. He was not a very satisfactory one because he went off on his own one day when he should have stayed with the Buddha—with rather disastrous consequences for himself.

Although the Buddha had had some difficulty in finding a satisfactory personal attendant, Ananda was by no means in a hurry to take on the task. It is as though he realized that it would be no easy matter to be the constant companion of an Enlightened one. Ananda had made steady progress in the spiritual life. He was certainly a 'Stream Entrant', he was irreversible from full Enlightenment. But he was not a Buddha. And even for someone like Ananda, even for a Stream Entrant, even for someone who had grown up with the Buddha, it was a rather awe-inspiring prospect to be the Buddha's constant companion, to be with him, by day and by night, in rain and in sun, year in and year out. Ananda therefore thought the matter over very carefully. He had seen some previous attendants come somewhat to grief, and was reluctant to give the Buddha any further trouble.

In the end, however, Ananda decided to accept the challenge, but laid down certain conditions, of which a couple are relevant here. One of these was that he should not be given any share in the various offerings and invitations that were given to the Buddha. He argued that, if people saw him benefiting from the offerings that were made to the Buddha—all the new robes and so on, then they might think that he was acting as the Buddha's companion just for the sake of what he could get out of it. He also realized that there would be times when he might have to be away from the Buddha, running errands, taking messages, and so on. While he was away, someone might come to see the Buddha and ask for a teaching. In consequence, the Buddha might give a discourse, might even give an important teaching, in his absence. So another condition he laid down was that the Buddha should repeat whatever teaching he had given during his absence.

The Buddha accepted these conditions, and Ananda became his constant companion for twenty years. How successful this arrangement was can be seen from an incident that occurred shortly before the Buddha's *Parinibbana*, his final passing away. Ananda was very deeply upset by the prospect of losing the Buddha. Apparently he stood leaning against the door, weeping. As he wept, he said: 'Alas, I am still a pupil with much to be done, and my Master will be passing utterly away, *he who was so kind to me.*' This was Ananda's impression of the Buddha after twenty years of constant, day to day, companionship. He did not say that the Buddha was *wise*, or *energetic*, but that the Buddha was *kind*.

Fortunately, we also know about the Buddha's impression of Ananda. For when he was told that Ananda was weeping outside, he sent for him and spoke the following words of encouragement:

> 'For many a long day, Ananda, the Tathagata has been waited on by you with kindly body-service, that is profitable, ease-giving, undivided, and unstinted; waited on with kindly service of speech, that is profitable, ease-giving, undivided, and unstinted; with kindly service of thought, that is profitable, ease-giving, undivided, and unstinted.'[*]

Thus the Buddha's predominant impression of Ananda was that he too was kind, that Ananda had served him with kindness of body, speech, and mind, that he had kept nothing back, that he had given himself totally. The relation between the Buddha and Ananda was essentially one of mutual kindness, even though the Buddha was spiritually by far the more developed of the two.

This may seem like a very small thing. But if we reflect we shall realize that it is actually a very big thing that they were kind to each other. Their kindness had never failed,

---

[*] *Ibid.* p.349

had never been found wanting even for a moment on either side. When two people are constant companions, and when the relation between them is of unfailing mutual kindness, you can only say of them that they are *friends*. Indeed, you can only say that they are *spiritual friends*, because such unfailing mutual kindness over such a long period of time is possible only on a deeply spiritual basis.

To some, it may seem a little strange that the Buddha and Ananda were friends. It may seem strange, perhaps, that the Buddha should have had a friend. One may wonder whether a Buddha *needs* a friend. But this depends on one's conception of Enlightenment. In response, I can give only a hint.

The Enlightenment experience is not self-contained in a one-sided way. The Enlightenment experience contains an element of 'communication', and contains, therefore, an element of spiritual friendship, even 'transcendental friendship', or friendship of the highest conceivable level. This, perhaps, is the significance of the Buddha's having a constant companion. There is surely no question of the Buddha keeping up the 'dignity' of a Buddha. Ananda is not a sort of spiritual valet-cum-private-secretary. The fact that he is 'in attendance', as the translator has it, represents the fact that there exists within the Enlightenment experience, within the heart of Reality, an element of communication, an element of spiritual friendship, something that found expression in the later history of Buddhist thought as that rather mysterious concept of *Sambhogakaya*.

The Exalted One was going his rounds of the lodgings, with the Venerable Ananda in attendance, and came to the lodging of that brother.

There is a second point to notice here: the Exalted One was going his rounds of the *lodgings*. In the original, the word for 'lodging' is *vihara*, and that is all that *vihara* really means. We must not imagine the Buddha going his rounds of a large, palatial, well-furnished monastery. The lodgings in question were probably just clusters of thatched huts scattered over an area of park-land just a few miles outside the city gates.

The Buddha was making his *rounds* of these lodgings. In other words, he was taking a personal interest in the monks. How were they getting on? What were they doing? How were they passing their time? There was of course no question of them sitting outside their thatched huts reading newspapers, or listening to transistor radios, or watching television. But they might possibly have been up to other things that they should not have been up to. They might have needed some encouragement, some teaching, or even a little ticking-off. The Buddha was seeing things for himself. In this way, he and Ananda came to the lodging of that brother.

Now the Exalted One saw that brother lying where he had fallen in his own excrements, and seeing him He went towards him, came to him, and said: 'Brother, what ails you?'

'I have dysentery, Lord.'

'But is there anyone taking care of you, brother?'

'No, Lord.'

'Why is it, brother, that the brethren do not take care of you?'

'I am useless to the brethren, Lord: therefore the brethren do not care for me.'

There are a number of points to be noted here. The Buddha goes towards the sick monk, asks him what is wrong with him, and gets very quickly to the heart of the matter. All of these points could be enlarged upon, but perhaps that is not necessary, their significance being sufficiently clear. The main point of this section is contained in the sick monk's last reply to the Buddha: 'I am useless to the brethren, Lord: therefore the brethren do not care for me.'

This is a very significant statement indeed. It is a shocking, terrible statement. Of course, we have only the bare words of the printed page to go by. We do not know how those words were spoken—and this can of course make a difference. Did the Buddha say 'Why is it brother that the brethren do not take care of you?' indignantly, or with concern, or sadly? And did the sick monk reply with dignity, with resignation, with weariness, or with bitterness and anger? We do not know. All we have is the bleak, shocking, statement itself, 'I am useless to the brethren, Lord: therefore the brethren do not care for me.'

However the words were spoken, they must imply, sadly, that people are interested in you only so long as you are useful to them, only so long as they can get something out of you. It implies that they see you not as a person but as a thing.

To treat a person as a thing is to treat them unethically. And this, apparently, is how the other monks were treating the sick monk. He was not useful to them, and so they were not interested in him. He was left lying in his own excrement. No one took care of him. There was no kindness between the sick monk and the other monks as there was between the Buddha and Ananda. There was no ordinary human friendship—not to speak of spiritual friendship; neither was there any sympathy or sensitivity or awareness. There could not be, because these are qualities that you can experience only in relation to a person whom you actually see as a person. The other monks did not see the sick monk as a person. To them he was like an old worn out broom, or a broken pot. He was useless to them so they did not care for him.

Only too often we ourselves can behave like this. We often consider people primarily in terms of their usefulness. We do this even within the Spiritual Community. Sometimes we are more interested in someone's talents and capacities—as a bricklayer, accountant, or lecturer—than in what they are in themselves. If you are treated in this way, then, when you are no longer able or willing to employ your talents, you may have the disappointing and disillusioning experience of finding that nobody wants to know you, nobody wants to be 'friends' with you any more. We must therefore learn to see persons as persons. There must be kindness between us, there must be spiritual friendship, as there was between the Buddha and Ananda. There must be sympathy, sensitivity, and awareness.

There are two principal aspects to persons treating each other as persons. These are communication and taking delight. These two are of the essence of friendship.

Even in the case of ordinary friendship there is the great benefit and blessing of being able to share our thoughts and feelings with another human being. It has been said that self-disclosure, the making of oneself known to another human being—being known by them and knowing that you are known by them—is essential to human health and happiness. If you are shut up in yourself, without any possibility of communication with another person, you don't stay healthy or happy for long.

In the case of spiritual friendship, we share our experience of the Dhamma itself. We share our enthusiasm, our inspiration, and our understanding. We even share our mistakes. Here, communication takes the form of confession.

The aspect of 'taking delight' means that we not only see a person as a person, but also *like* what we see, enjoy and take delight in what we see, just as we do with a beautiful painting or poem—except that here the painting or poem is alive: the painting can speak to you, and the beautiful

71

poem can answer back! This makes it very exciting and stimulating indeed. Here we see, we like, we love and appreciate a person entirely for their own sake, and not for the sake of anything useful that we can get out of them. This also happens in ordinary friendship to some extent, but it happens to a far greater extent in spiritual friendship—*kalyana mitrata*. The primary meaning of *kalyana* is 'beautiful'. In spiritual friendship we take delight in the *spiritual* beauty of our friend: we rejoice in his or her merits.

> Then the Exalted One said to the venerable Ananda: 'Go you, Ananda, and fetch water. We will wash this brother.'
>
> 'Yes, Lord,' replied the venerable Ananda to the Exalted One. When he had fetched the water, the Exalted One poured it out, while the venerable Ananda washed that brother all over. Then the Exalted One taking him by the head and the venerable Ananda taking him by the feet, together they laid him on the bed.

There are a number of significant points here. The Buddha acts *instantly*. As a human being he seems to have been of a prompt, decisive, character, not unlike a military commander. At this stage he does not ask anyone how it all happened, but simply sends Ananda off for water. Then, the Buddha and Ananda act *together*. Ananda does not argue with the Buddha; they don't have a long discussion as to who should pour the water and who should wash the sick man, or who should take him by the head and who should take him by the feet. They act together harmoniously, efficiently, and effectively.

Perhaps more importantly, the Buddha and Ananda *accept responsibility* for the situation, even though it is not of their making. They do not try to hand the responsibility

over to anybody else, but take care of the sick monk themselves, doing whatever needs to be done. They make the
sick monk comfortable, and only then does the Buddha call
the other monks together:

> Then the Exalted One, in this connexion and on this
> occasion, gathered the Order of Brethren together,
> and questioned the brethren, saying:
> 'Brethren, is there in such and such a lodging a
> brother who is sick?'
> 'There is, Lord.'
> 'And what ails that brother?'
> 'Lord, that brother has dysentery.'
> 'But, brethren, is there anyone taking care of him?'
> 'No, Lord.'
> 'Why not? Why do not the brethren take care of
> him?'
> 'That brother is useless to the brethren, Lord. That
> is why the brethren do not take care of him.'

There are two points here. First, the Buddha looks into the
matter. He does not jump to conclusions. He does not
immediately assume that the other monks are guilty of
deliberate neglect. He first ascertains the facts of the case,
giving the other monks an opportunity to explain, even to
defend themselves. He gives them an opportunity to *con-
fess*—and that is what they do.

This is an important lesson. So often we jump to conclusions; we assume that someone is guilty before we have
ascertained all the facts. When we don't get a reply to a
letter we assume that the person to whom we have written
has not replied and conclude that he is not being a good
friend. We then write a second, angry, letter. But surely we
should first ascertain that our friend did actually *receive* the
letter. And we should make sure that he has not in fact
replied. Only then should we adopt whatever course seems

appropriate.

This is just what the Buddha did, with the result that the monks confessed their mistake. I say that they confessed, but one does rather get the impression from this passage that they did not realize that there was anything wrong with their behaviour. If this was the case, then they must have had a very inadequate conception of the spiritual life, of the spiritual community, and of spiritual friendship. Be that as it may, once they had confessed, the Buddha could exhort them thus:

'Brethren, ye have no mother and no father to take care of you. If ye will not take care of each other, who else, I ask, will do so? Brethren, he who would wait on me, let him wait on the sick.

Here, the Buddha is laying down an important set of principles. He is asserting an absolute discontinuity between the biological family and the 'spiritual family', between the 'group' and the 'spiritual community'. Once you enter the spiritual community you no longer belong to the group, and you no longer rely upon it. The Buddha does not mean that your mother and father are dead in the literal sense. He means that *spiritually speaking* they no longer exist. In other words, they no longer exist as your mother and father. You can therefore no longer depend upon them to take care of you, no longer take *refuge* in them.

This is what is meant by the 'Going Forth'. It is a going forth 'from home into homelessness'. You go forth from the group to the spiritual community. Spiritually speaking, the group no longer exists. And since it no longer exists, you no longer rely on it or take refuge in it.

Once you enter the spiritual community, only the spiritual community exists. You take refuge solely in the Three Jewels: the Buddha, the Dhamma, and the Sangha. You rely only on other members of the spiritual community, and that means that other members of the spiritual community rely on you. You rely on one another, take care of one another, encourage one another, and inspire one another.

All of this certainly applies to our own spiritual community, the Western Buddhist Order. We have in fact no mother and no father to take care of us. What was formerly done by our family must now be done by our spiritual friends—indeed *more* must be done by our spiritual friends.

But suppose it is not done? Suppose someone is ill, or depressed, or experiencing psychological difficulties, or not finding the spiritual life very enjoyable. If that person is left, as the sick monk was left, he may drift back to the group, back to the family, back to mother, wife, or girlfriend. He may go in search of comfort and consolation elsewhere.

It is important that as members of the spiritual community we realize that we have no true refuge except one another, no friends except one another—that is, no *real* friends except spiritual friends. From the group we can expect absolutely nothing—nor should we. We belong *absolutely* to the spiritual community, belong absolutely to one another. We should be prepared, therefore, to live and die for one another—otherwise we have not really gone for Refuge. Our future is with one another; we are one another's future; we have no future apart from one another.

The Buddha says, 'If ye will not take care of each other, who else, I ask, will do so?' If Order members do not love one another, who else will love them? If Order members do not inspire one another, who else will inspire them? If Order members cannot be happy with one another, who else can they be happy with? If they cannot come together with one another, who else can they come together with? Perhaps we should enjoy one another's company more,

75

appreciate one another more, value one another more.

The Buddha certainly valued the brethren highly. He says, 'Brethren, he who would wait on me, let him wait on the sick.' The Buddha is not being mystical or metaphysical here: he is dealing with the realities of life in the spiritual community. By 'the sick', he means sick *brethren*—fellow members of the spiritual community. If one wants to wait upon the Buddha, one should wait upon them. Thus the Buddha in a sense equates members of the spiritual community with himself. It would hardly be possible to value them more highly than that.

'If he have a teacher, let his teacher take care of him, so long as he is alive, and wait for his recovery. If he have a tutor or a lodger, a disciple or a fellow-lodger or a fellow-disciple, such should take care of him and await his recovery.' Thus all conceivable relationships within the spiritual community are covered. Teacher should take care of pupil, and pupil of teacher; fellow disciple should take care of fellow disciple; occupants of the same *vihara* (the same residential spiritual community) should take care of one another. In sickness and in health there should be unfailing kindness and spiritual friendship between them.

'If no one take care of him, it shall be reckoned an offence'. Here, 'offence' means an unskilful action that needs to be confessed. The responsibility for the care of each member rests on the entire spiritual community. Ultimately, all are responsible for each, and each is responsible for all to the extent of his strength. Otherwise there can be no spiritual community.

By now it should be clear that this story is not just about a sick monk being neglected by the brethren. It is not just a simple case of diarrhoea. It is a case of unfailing mutual kindness, a case of personal interest, a case of harmonious and effective action, a case of treating persons as persons, a case of communication and taking delight, a case of recognizing the absolute discontinuity between the group and the spiritual community. Above all it is a case of mutual responsibility and mutual spiritual friendship. Is is not a case of something that happened in the past, two-thousand-five-hundred years ago; it is a case of something that is happening *now*, in the present, and something that will happen in the future. It is not a case of something that concerned the ancient brethren; it is something that concerns their modern successors, ourselves.

Between the Twin Sala Trees

There are many Buddhist scriptures: in Pali, in Sanskrit, in Tibetan, in Chinese, and so on. There are also many Buddhist traditions: Theravada, Sarvastivada, Mahayana, and Vajrayana. And there are very many Buddhist teachings: about the cosmos, about meditation, about the mind, about mental states, about the nature of reality, about different kinds of living beings, about ethics—both personal and social, teachings even about the arts. In fact, there are so many scriptures, traditions, and teachings that one can sometimes get a little bewildered. Sometimes one might think how wonderful it would be if only all those books could be reduced to just one slim pocket volume that one could carry about all the time. How wonderful it would be if one could reduce those multitudinous chapters to just one chapter, all those verses to just one verse, or even reduce all those millions of words to just one magic word upon which alone one could ponder and continually reflect, knowing that if one did so one would be certain of gaining Enlightenment!

I have sometimes thought that this *could* be done, that perhaps all the teachings could be reduced to one teaching, in fact to just one magic, meaningful, word. That word would be 'impermanence'.

In a way, the whole of the Buddha's teaching is contained in that word. If you can understand impermanence it is almost as if you will understand everything that the Buddha ever said. It is not surprising, therefore, that we are told that the trees and birds in Sukhavati* have nothing else to say, nothing else to sing, than *anitya* (impermanence), *anatta* (selflessness), and *dukkha* (unsatisfactoriness). One might say that *anitya*, impermanence, would be sufficient since the other two principles are really contained in it. If we understand this one word, impermanence, in sufficient depth, we will see that the whole of the Buddha's teaching, both practical and theoretical, is implied therein.

We very often find, especially in the earlier portions of the Pali scriptures, that this insight into impermanence is expressed in terms of the realization that whatever has a beginning has an end, that whatever is born must die. If something has a beginning—and of course everything conditioned has a beginning—it must inevitably have an end. Sometimes this is expressed even more precisely and philosophically in the sentence: 'Whatever has by nature an origin, that also by nature has an end.' The end is not accidental, not grafted on: the end is inherent in something inasmuch as it has a beginning. Its beginning *is* its end; the fact that it is a 'beginning-thing' means that it is also an 'ending-thing'. If you are a 'born-thing', you are a 'dying-thing'.

In traditional Buddhist language, this realization is known as 'the opening of the Eye of Truth', or *Dhamma-Chakkhu* in Pali (Sanskrit *Dharma-Chakshu*). The opening of the Dhamma-Eye, the realization of the truth that whatever has by nature an origin has also by nature an end, is equivalent to Stream Entry. From this fact alone, we can appreciate the great importance of the opening of the Dhamma-Eye.

In the course of the *Vinaya-Pitaka* of the Pali Canon we meet Kondanna, one of the Buddha's first five disciples. It

---

* The Buddha Amitabha's Pure Land: according to some Mahayana schools, a sort of heavenly realm

is in connection with him that we hear of the Eye of Truth for the first time. Kondanna had been one of the Buddha's companions earlier on in his career, when the Buddha was practising severe asceticism and self-mortification. When the Buddha gave up that extreme path, Kondanna, like the Buddha's other four companions at that time, left him in disgust and wandered off. The Buddha too went off by himself, and eventually gained Enlightenment.

After gaining Enlightenment, the Buddha thought first of sharing his discovery with his old teachers, but realized that they were now dead. He then thought of his old companions, and realized that they were staying at the Deer Park, at Isipatana, in Sarnarth. So he went to them and, as the story goes, although they had determined not to show him any respect, they were quite unable to stop themselves from doing so when he actually arrived. The Buddha then sat down and talked with them.

They talked for an entire rainy season, the Buddha trying to get his old companions to see the truth that he had seen. This no easy task. He argued and expostulated; they discussed things vigorously. In the end the Buddha broke through and was able to communicate what he had been trying for so long to communicate. The first to realize that truth was this same Kondanna. He was the first among those five to get a glimpse of Enlightenment. The text says that when the Buddha had finished speaking, the 'pure and stainless Eye of Truth, the *Dhamma-Chakkhu*, arose in Kondanna,' and he realized that everything that has by nature an origin has also by nature a cessation.' In one overwhelming flash of insight, he realized the truth of impermanence.

At this point the text has a very interesting comment: 'Thus was the Wheel of the Dhamma set going by the Blessed One'. In other words, it had not really been set going until there was at least one Stream Entrant in the world. Before that the Buddha had been doing his utmost to communicate the Dhamma in words, and maybe in other ways too; but he had not actually set the Wheel of the Dhamma in motion. The Buddha had not really *taught* until there was one Stream Entrant in the world.

When this happened, when Kondanna had this great insight and the Buddha *saw* that he had had this great insight—that they shared one and the same insight between them—he was overjoyed. No longer would he have to keep his discovery to himself; it was now, to some extent at least, common property. At that moment, we are told, he let forth an *udana*, an inspired utterance, a song of ecstasy: 'Kondanna has understood! Kondanna has understood!' The Wheel of the Dhamma had been set rolling, and even he could not see where it would stop. Henceforth Kondanna was called *Annata*-Kondanna, 'Kondanna who has understood'.

It is interesting to note that the text says nothing about any further attainment beyond the opening of the Dhamma-Eye. It simply says of Kondanna that 'having attained the Dhamma, having understood the Dhamma, having immersed himself in the Dhamma, having left uncertainty behind, having escaped from doubt, having attained confidence and not dependent on others in the doctrine of the teacher, he asked for ordination.'[*] And this the Buddha granted. We are told the same thing about all four of the remaining ascetics. In their cases the Buddha had a little more difficulty in breaking through, but he managed in the end. In their cases too the Dhamma-Eye arose; they too saw that everything that has by nature an origin has also by nature a cessation. They too asked for ordination, and they too were ordained. In all these cases it was the opening of the Dhamma-Eye that seems to have

---

[*] Vinaya Pitaka, *Mahavagga* I, 6, 31, trans. Nanamoli

been the real turning point.

Let us therefore return to impermanence. Impermanence is all around us. Everything is impermanent; there is nothing that is not. We see the leaves fall and the flowers fade; everything is impermanent. But the most vivid and the most powerful form in which we encounter impermanence is in death, the dissolution of the physical body—especially in the death of someone near and dear to us.

Buddhism offers a number of practices which are intended to remind us of death, to remind us that, inasmuch as the physical body was 'put' together, one day it is going to fall apart.

There is, for instance, the Six Element practice (or at least the first four stages of that Six Element practice). Here, we reflect that whatever there is in us of the earth element is borrowed from the earth element which exists all around us in the universe. One day we will have to give it back. Similarly with the water element, the fire element, and with the air element: one day we are going to have to give them all back. That process of giving back, willingly or unwillingly, is the process of dissolution of the physical body, or death.

Then there are the ten so-called 'corpse meditations'. Here, you go along to a cremation, or charnel, ground, and see corpses in various stages of decomposition. You then reflect that as they are, so too will you be one day, because you too are subject to death.

Then again, there is the relatively straightforward practice of the simple recollection of death. Here you just remind yourself that one day you will have to die, just as every other human being will have to die.

These practices all serve to remind us that human beings are subject to death: all must one day die. Even the greatest, even the best, even great heroes, must die—their power does not save them. Great artists and poets must die—their art and poetry does not save them. Sometimes these people die premature, even unpleasant, deaths. One thinks of Keats dying of consumption at twenty-five, of Shelley, drowned at thirty, one thinks—in Wordsworth's phrase— of 'mighty poets in their misery dead'. One thinks of Spinoza, a great philosopher, again dying of consumption at the age of about forty. They all die sooner or later, prematurely or in the ripeness of their years. Their political greatness, moral greatness, artistic greatness, philosophical greatness cannot save them.

Even the Buddha had to die. The Buddha was Enlightened, but he was an Enlightened *human being*, and every human being must die because every human being was born. Everything that has a beginning must have an end. It may seem strange that a Buddha should have to die, but inasmuch as he is human, or to the extent that he is human, he must die.

The *Mahaparinibbana Sutta* is the sixteenth *sutta* of the *Digha Nikaya* and gives an account of the last few months, and especially the last day—or rather night—of the Buddha's earthly existence. It is a composite work consisting of a number of different episodes and teachings. I would like to investigate four episodes from this *sutta*. These are the episode of the Mirror of the Dhamma, the episode of the teaching of 'subjective' and 'objective' Refuge, the episode of the Untimely Flowers, and the episode of the Last Disciple. The first two episodes took place on the road to Kusinara, and the second two took place at Kusinara, or rather just outside Kusinara, in the sala grove of the Mallas—between the twin sala trees.

The episode of the Mirror of the Dhamma involves Ananda; in fact, all four episodes involve Ananda in one way or another, because Ananda accompanied the Buddha on his last journey and was present at the Parinibbana itself. Ananda emerges from the Pali scriptures as a vivid and lovable personality. He also seems to have had a very inquisitive mind—as we shall see.

The episode took place at a little place called Nadika, where the Buddha was staying at the 'Brick Hall'. The Buddha had a large number of disciples in that area, so no sooner had the Buddha and Ananda settled down than Ananda went off to visit them. On his return he told the Buddha that a *bhikkhu* and a *bhikkhuni*, as well as quite a number of lay disciples, had all died since their last visit. Having an inquisitive mind, however, Ananda was not content just to give the Buddha this information; he wanted to know about the *destiny* of those deceased people. Where had they been reborn? Had they even been reborn at all? The Buddha—and one can imagine him heaving a sort of sigh here—tells Ananda what he wants to know.

It seems that quite a lot of people have died, so the Buddha's account takes rather a long time. When he has finished, he tells Ananda that it is becoming wearisome to have to go into this sort of thing every time someone dies. He therefore says that he will teach him how to work these things out for himself. He will teach him the Mirror of the Dhamma.

Although there is much that could be said about the Mirror of the Dhamma itself, I am actually concerned here with another point—one that arises in connection with this teaching. I am concerned with the number of *lay* disciples in that place who had, according to the Buddha, become 'Non-Returners', 'Once Returners', and 'Stream Entrants'. The Buddha tells Ananda that the *bhikkhu*, having become an arahat, would not be reborn at all; the *bhikkhuni* had become a Non-Returner; one lay disciple had become a Once-Returner; one lay disciple had become a Stream Entrant. Then, he says, there were fifty-seven more lay disciples who had become Non-Returners, more than ninety who had become Once-Returners, and more than five hundred who had become Stream Entrants—all in one place, and all apparently since the Buddha's last visit.

All this clearly suggests that Stream Entry, at least, is not such a very rare occurrence as is generally supposed. On the strength of this passage alone, we must conclude that Stream Entry is well within the reach of the serious-minded practising Buddhist, whether living as a 'monk' or 'nun', or as a lay person.

Now comes the episode, or teaching, of 'subjective' and 'objective' refuge. The Buddha and his monk-disciples customarily spent eight or nine months of each year wandering from place to place. Then, for the duration of the rainy season, they would settle in one place. On this particular occasion, they stayed for the three months of the rainy season at the village of Beluva.

While they were staying there, perhaps because it was the rainy season, the Buddha became very ill. However, thinking that it would not be right for him to pass away without taking leave of the order, he made a strong effort of will and suppressed his sickness. He had been staying during this time in a *vihara*, a lodging—probably a little cottage with no more than one room. On his recovery he came outside and sat in the shade, perhaps just enjoying the fresh air and sunshine.

As he sat there, Ananda came up to him. Ananda was quite disturbed by the thought of the Buddha's passing away, so the Buddha took advantage of this opportunity to make certain points, and to give him certain exhortations. In the actual words of the scripture, the Buddha said: 'Therefore, in this regard, Ananda, abide self-reliant (*attadipa*), taking refuge in yourself, not taking refuge in others, reliant on the Dhamma, taking refuge in the

Dhamma, not taking refuge in another.'* This was the Buddha's exhortation.

There seems to be a sort of contradiction here. On the one hand one is being asked to take refuge in oneself—and on the other hand one is being asked to take refuge in the Dhamma. On the one hand there is what I call 'subjective refuge', and on the other there is what I call 'objective refuge'.

Unfortunately, the passage which immediately follows does not help us very much. Here the Buddha simply says that one takes refuge in the self *and* in the Dhamma by the practice of the four foundations of mindfulness, the four *satipatannas*: mindfulness of the physical body, mindfulness of sensations, mindfulness of thoughts, and mindfulness of *dhammas* (*dhammas* here meaning: mental objects, doctrinal categories or realities). In this way, apparently, the subjective and objective refuges are to be reconciled.

But, to go a little further than this, we could say that 'subjective refuge' represents thinking of the spiritual life in terms of personal—or individual—development, while 'objective refuge' represents thinking of the spiritual life in terms of devotion to a supremely worthwhile *object*. Actually, we have to have both, and we have to hold them in balance.

In our own movement that balance is possibly tilted in favour of the subjective refuge—though I think that this has started to change. We tend to think in terms of something being good for one's own personal spiritual development, in a rather 'precious' sort of way. We tend, perhaps, to ignore the needs of the objective situation. One hears, for instance, of people not attending some business meetings because they don't feel in an 'organizational mood' that morning. Going to the meeting, they seem to think, would

---
* Digha Nikaya 16

be detrimental to their spiritual development. However, as I have said, this has started changing, and people's approach is beginning to be rather more balanced. More weight is being given to the needs of the objective situation, more weight is being given to the Buddhas and Bodhisattvas, more weight is being given to other people.

Thirdly, we have the episode of the 'Untimely Flowers'. This episode took place in the sala grove near Kusinara, and it took place, as did the succeeding episode, between the twin sala trees. Let us try to visualize the scene.

The Mallas, the tribal people in whose territory Kusinara was situated, had planted two parallel rows of sala trees, running from east to west. At the eastern end of the two rows, between the last two trees, was a kind of platform which was apparently used for meetings. The Buddha lay down upon this with his head to the north and his feet to the south. Lying down, as he usually did, on his right side, his head to the north and his feet to the south, he would have been facing west, looking right down the great avenue of sala trees. Had you been walking up this avenue, you would have seen the Buddha lying between the last two sala trees right at the very end—a very impressive sight.

We should perhaps note that the Buddha passed away in the open air. According to tradition the Buddha was also born in the open air, gained Enlightenment in open air, and often taught in the open air. In other words, he lived very close to nature throughout his life.

While the Buddha was lying between the twin sala trees, something strange happened. The Buddha himself drew Ananda's attention to it. Here are the exact words of the Pali text:

Then said the Exalted One to the venerable Ananda:
  'See, Ananda! All abloom are the twin Sala trees:

with untimely blossoms do they shower down on the body of the Tathagata, they sprinkle it, cover it up, in worship of the Tathagata. Moreover, heavenly frankincense comes falling from the sky, showers down upon the body of the Tathagata, sprinkles it and covers it up, in worship of the Tathagata. And heavenly music sounds in the sky, in worship of the Tathagata, and heavenly songs are wafted from the sky in worship of the Tathagata.

Yet not thus is the Tathagata truly honoured, revered, respected, worshipped, and deferred to. Whosoever, Ananda, be he brother or sister, or lay-brother or lay-sister,—whosoever dwells in the fulfil-ment of the Dhamma, both in its greater and in its lesser duties,—whosoever walks uprightly in accord-ance with the Dhamma,—he it is that truly honours, reveres, respects, worships, and defers to the Tathagata in the perfection of worship.'

Although the heart of the matter seems to be that true worship of the Buddha consists in the practice of his teach-ing, there is a danger of a misunderstanding. The passage seems to fit in very neatly with our Western, rationalistic way of thinking, our rationalistic pre-suppositions. The passage might seem to be saying that the offering of flowers, lights, and candles is unnecessary. But this is not what the passage is saying at all.

It is true that the offering of flowers and so on is by no means any substitute for the actual practice of the Buddha's teaching: the practice of morality (*sila*), the practice of meditation (*samadhi*), and the practice of wisdom (*panna*). But this does not mean that we should not offer those flowers. Offering flowers is an expression of devotion and thus *strengthens* devotion. If we do not feel any devotion

---

* *Ibid.* p.347

then we will probably not practise the teaching.

We must also remember whom the Buddha was addressing. Ananda seems to have been an emotional rather than intellectual type of person. Perhaps he was sometimes carried away by his feelings and needed to be reminded that feelings, even devotional feelings, were not everything.

Our position in the modern West is quite different. Many of us find it quite easy to *understand* the Dhamma; we even find it easy to practise it up to a point. But we find it very difficult to experience strong devotional feelings. Some of us hardly know what devotional feelings are—they are just things we hear or read about! As a consequence, sooner or later, our spiritual life comes to a halt, or at least stagnates very badly. Unlike Ananda, and unlike those sala trees, we actually need to offer all the flowers we can, even great armfuls of them. We should certainly not take this passage as condoning a purely rationalistic attitude to spiritual life.

Finally, we have the episode of 'the Last Disciple'. The name of this last person to be 'converted' by the Buddha himself was Subhadda. Subhadda was a wanderer, a *paribbajaka*, and just happened to be in the vicinity of Kusinara when he heard that the Buddha was about to pass away. Thinking that he should not miss such an opportunity, he came to where the Buddha was staying.

Ananda, not wishing the Buddha to be disturbed at such a time, would not allow him to get close enough to the Buddha to speak with him. Overhearing their conversation, however, the Buddha asked Ananda to let Subhadda approach, and the Buddha and Subhadda entered into conversation. The Buddha taught, and Subhadda was, as we might say, 'converted'. Being converted, he went for Refuge, asked for ordination.

Here we are concerned with just one point, a point not actually mentioned in the text itself, but in

Buddhaghosha's commentary to the *sutta*. The text speaks of the Buddha granting Subhadda's request for ordination by telling Ananda: 'Ordain him'. The commentary then tells us exactly how this was done: what Ananda did, and what the Buddha did on that occasion. This is very important, because it is clearly based on a very ancient tradition. Here is the passage:

> The Thera (Ananda), they say, took him (Subhadda) on one side, poured water over his head from a water vessel, made him repeat the formula of meditation on the impermanency of the body, shaved off his hair and beard, clad him in the yellow robes, made him repeat the Three Refuges, and led him back to the Exalted One. The Exalted One himself admitted him then into the higher rank of the brotherhood, and pointed out to him a subject for meditation. *

This is particularly interesting because there is a distinct parallel with our own ordination procedure in the Western Buddhist Order. According to Buddhagosha, Subhadda is first made to go for Refuge, then he is given a meditation subject, his hair and beard are shaved, water is poured over his head, he is clad in yellow robes, and, finally, he is accepted into the ranks of the Sangha. All of these elements, except one, are found in our own private and public ordination ceremonies.

First of all there is the Going for Refuge. This is found in both the private ceremony and the public ceremony. Then there is the giving of a subject for meditation; this is found in the private ordination ceremony when one is given a visualization and mantra recitation practice. Thirdly comes the shaving of hair and beard. This is not found in

---

* from Buddhagosha's commentary to the *Parinibbanasuttanta*, *Digha Nikaya ii*, 153

the case of the Western Buddhist Order (though some men do sometimes have a very close crop just before ordination). Then comes the pouring of the water; that is found in our public ordination ceremony. Fifthly, being clad in yellow robes corresponds to the investiture with the *kesa** found in the public ordination ceremony. Sixthly and lastly, of course, one's reception into the ranks of the Sangha occurs in the course of the public ordination ceremony.

There is thus only one item that is not found in our own ordination procedure, and just one item in our own ordination procedure which is not present in Subhadda's case: the giving of a new name.

All this is quite significant in view of the fact that, in the FWBO and in the WBO, we try to go back to the origins of things, try to base ourselves on what is fundamental in the Buddhist tradition. It is of further interest that T. W. Rhys-Davids, the translator of the *Digha-Nikaya*, has a judicious note on this commentarial passage: 'According to this, no set ceremony for ordination (*Sangha-kammam*), as laid down in the Vinaya [which of course developed some time later], took place; and it is otherwise probable that no such ceremony was usual in the earliest days of Buddhism.'** The implications of this statement demand to be very well pondered indeed.

The day on which we commemorate the 'great passing away', or *Mahaparinibbana*, of the Buddha, is one of the major Buddhist festivals of the year. In recent years, however, I do not believe that we in the FWBO have paid as much attention to this occasion as perhaps we could have done. I would therefore like to conclude this talk by making a few suggestions as to how the day might be marked.

Firstly, if at all possible, we should observe the

---

* a strip of white silk emblazoned with a Three Jewels motif
** Ibid.

Parinibbana Day throughout the day. We should read the *Mahaparinibbana Sutta* aloud in the shrine room, and chant the Vajrasattva Mantra. It is perhaps not necessary to read through the *Mahaparinibbana Sutta* in its entirety on this occasion; one could read only those sections which have a direct bearing on the events leading up the Parinibbana itself.

The chanting of the Vajrasattva mantra could be performed at intervals throughout the day. But why the hundred syllable mantra of Vajrasattva? Why not the mantra of Tara, or Manjushri, or Vajrapani, or Padmasambhava? The answer is quite simple. Vajrasattva is connected with death. The manner in which I first discovered this takes me back to 1958 or '59, when I was living in Kalimpong.

On one occasion I went up to Gangtok, the capital of Sikkim, to see Jamyang Khyentse Rimpoche, who was one of my Tibetan teachers. He was staying at the Palace Temple, on the outskirts of Gangtok. Upon arriving I was ushered into an antechamber and asked to wait for about half an hour. When I was ushered into his presence he received me, as always, in a very kindly and fatherly sort of way, and apologised for having kept me waiting—adding, by way of explanation, that he had been performing the Vajrasattva puja and recitation of the Vajrasattva mantra on behalf of a lama friend who had just died. As he talked a little more about this, I came to understand that Vajrasattva was connected with death.

A few years later, in the winter of 1966–67, I had a rather strange experience in this connection. I was back in Kalimpong, having spent two years in the West. By now I had decided to settle in England, and was in Kalimpong on a farewell visit, staying at my Triyana Vardhana Vihara.

One night I woke up at about two o'clock in the morning. I really did wake up—this was not a dream or a vision.

Everything was bright as if I was in daylight. I sat up on my bed and, looking down towards the side of my bed, I saw a great pit in the floor that certainly had not been there the previous evening. I looked down into the pit. Standing there was an old friend—one who had been dead for several years.

The pit must have been just over six feet deep because he was about six feet tall and was completely contained in the pit. For some minutes I just looked. I knew that he was dead, of course. I also knew that something was wrong and that something had to be done. But what? That was when I thought of Jamyang Khyentse Rimpoche and what he had told me about the Vajrasattva Mantra.

Sitting up on my bed, I started repeating the Vajrasattva mantra. As I did so, the words of the mantra—in Tibetan characters—came out of my mouth. They came out of my mouth and formed a sort of garland, or chain, which went right down into the pit and then looped back up again—just within reach of the person in the pit. My friend caught hold of this garland, and so pulled himself out of the pit. He then disappeared.

At that moment I suddenly heard horns being blown just outside. Only then did I remember that it was the night of the new moon and that the Jogis were abroad. The Jogis are a particular caste or sect of the Nepalese, a very strange people. A hereditary duty has been imposed upon them to go around at certain times of the year, on the night of the new moon, to collect the souls of the dead. The Nepalese people keep away from them. Dogs keep away from them too—even the fiercest dog will not touch them. In the morning they come to the houses that they have been clearing of spirits, and you are supposed to give them a little raw rice and some money. Most Nepalese people are so afraid they just throw the money and rice to them from a distance and retreat as quickly as they can.

Since that experience I have had a certain amount of faith in the Vajrasattva mantra in this connection. Vajrasattva is associated not only with death, but with 'hell'—not hell in the Christian sense, of course, but in the sense of lower states of temporary suffering. And Vajrasattva is perhaps associated with hell because he is associated with death, at least so far as 'ordinary' people are concerned, people—that is to say—who have not attained Stream Entry.

To return to the observance of Parinirvana Day, the day should be an occasion for remembering not just the Buddha's Parinirvana, but also other deceased persons, especially Order members, mitras, and Friends who have died in the course of the previous year or so. We can perhaps place their photographs on the shrine, below images of Buddhas, Bodhisattvas, and gurus. Their full names and the dates of their death should be read out either during or before a Sevenfold Puja*. We can also commemorate the friends and relations of Order members, mitras, and Friends. If anybody wants to bring along the photograph, or hand in the name, of anybody near and dear to them who has died, especially during the course of the past year, they should be free to do that.

There are a number of positive reasons for this suggestion. First of all, the significance of the Parinirvana Day itself will be enhanced. Secondly, we will be reminded that everyone dies, whether Enlightened or unenlightened. Thirdly, in the case of deceased Order members especially, we will be reminded that physical death does not interrupt the spiritual connection. The spiritual community, in the broadest sense, consists of both the 'living' and the 'dead'. In this way we shall be helped to transcend the limitations of the physical body, enabled to realize that the spiritual

---

* A collective devotional practice usually performed at the end of a day's events

community is not limited by space and time, and that, in a sense, the dead are not really dead. Fourthly, a commemoration of this sort will help bereaved Order members, mitras, Friends, and others to come to terms with the fact of death, and come to terms with the fact that they have lost, as it seems, someone near and dear to them. Fifthly, commemorating other people who have recently died will help to remind us that, inasmuch as we may be separated from those near and dear to us at any moment, we should compose our quarrels.

One sometimes hears people saying, 'I am so sad, not just that the person has died, but that we could not resolve a certain misunderstanding before they died.' It might have been one's father or mother, one's brother or sister, or a friend, or a fellow Order member or mitra, but you feel sorry that that breach, that wound, has not been healed and that the person has died without the two of you having been reconciled. Death may come at any time; it does not always give advance warning. So if there is any misunderstanding unresolved, we should settle it immediately.

In ten days time we shall be observing that anniversary of the Buddha's Parinibbana. I hope that what I have said here will, among other things, help to make it an even more significant occasion than usual. I hope that it will give us an even deeper insight into the truth of impermanence. I hope it will give an even deeper realization of the inevitability of death. I hope it will enable us to be 'present' with the Buddha on that occasion, between the twin sala trees.